SAUDI ARABIA 2016 HUMAN RIGHTS REPORT

EXECUTIVE SUMMARY

The Kingdom of Saudi Arabia is a monarchy ruled by King Salman bin Abdulaziz Al Saud, who is both head of state and head of government. The government bases its legitimacy on its interpretation of sharia (Islamic law) and the 1992 Basic Law, which specifies that the rulers of the country shall be male descendants of the founder, King Abdulaziz bin Abdulrahman Al Saud. The Basic Law sets out the system of governance, rights of citizens, and powers and duties of the government, and it provides that the Quran and Sunna (the traditions of the Prophet Muhammad) serve as the country's constitution. In December 2015 the country held municipal elections on a nonparty basis for two-thirds of the 3,159 seats on the 284 municipal councils around the country. Independent polling station observers identified no significant irregularities with the election. For the first time, women were allowed to vote and run as candidates.

Civilian authorities generally maintained effective control over the security forces.

The most important human rights problems reported included citizens' lack of the ability and legal means to choose their government; restrictions on universal rights, such as freedom of expression, including on the internet, and the freedoms of assembly, association, movement, and religion; and pervasive gender discrimination and lack of equal rights that affected most aspects of women's lives.

Other human rights problems reported included: a lack of judicial independence and transparency that manifested itself in denial of due process and arbitrary arrest and detention; a lack of equal rights for children and noncitizen workers; abuses of detainees; overcrowding in prisons and detention centers; investigating, detaining, prosecuting, and sentencing lawyers, human rights activists, and antigovernment reformists; holding political prisoners; arbitrary interference with privacy, home, and correspondence; and a lack of equal rights for children and noncitizen workers. Violence against women; trafficking in persons; and discrimination based on gender, religion, sect, race, and ethnicity were common. Lack of governmental transparency and access made it difficult to assess the magnitude of many reported human rights problems.

The government identified, prosecuted, and punished a limited number of officials who committed abuses, particularly those engaged or complicit in corruption.

Some members of the security forces and other senior officials reportedly committed abuses with relative impunity.

The country continued air and ground operations in Yemen as leader of a military coalition formed in March 2015 to counter the 2014 overthrow of the internationally recognized Republic of Yemen government in Sana'a by Houthi rebels allied with forces loyal to former president Ali Abdullah Saleh. Saudi-led coalition airstrikes in Yemen resulted in civilian casualties and damage to infrastructure on multiple occasions, and the United Nations and nongovernmental organizations (NGOs), such as Human Rights Watch (HRW) and Amnesty International, claimed that some coalition airstrikes were disproportionate or indiscriminate and appeared not to sufficiently minimize collateral impact on civilians. Houthi-Saleh militias conducted cross-border raids into Saudi territory and fired missiles and artillery into southern Saudi Arabia throughout the year, killing Saudi civilians. The coalition's Joint Incident Assessment Team, established by the government and based in Riyadh, investigated some incidents of coalition airstrikes that reportedly resulted in civilian casualties and published recommendations, although no prosecutions resulted.

Section 1. Respect for the Integrity of the Person, Including Freedom from:

a. Arbitrary Deprivation of Life and other Unlawful or Politically Motivated Killings

There was one allegation that the government or its agents committed arbitrary or unlawful killings within the country. On March 3, Makki al-Orayedh died while in police custody after police detained him on March 1 at a checkpoint in Awamiya. On March 5, the European Saudi Organization for Human Rights (ESOHR) claimed police tortured al-Orayedh to death. According to ESOHR, authorities claimed al-Orayedh died due to "a psychological state of fear." Local media did not report on whether authorities investigated his death.

Under the country's interpretation and practice of sharia, capital punishment can be imposed for a range of nonviolent offenses, including apostasy, sorcery, and adultery, although in practice death sentences for such offenses were rare and often reduced on appeal. The law requires a five-judge appellate court to affirm a death sentence, which then must be unanimously affirmed by the Supreme Judicial Council; defendants are generally able to appeal their sentences. Closed court proceedings in some capital cases, however, made it impossible to determine whether authorities allowed the accused to present a defense or afforded minimum due process rights. Since the country lacks a written penal code listing criminal offenses and the associated penalties for them (see section 1.e.), punishment--including the imposition of capital punishment--is subject to considerable judicial discretion in the courts. In addition, there is no right under the law to seek a pardon or commutation of a death sentence for all crimes. The law of criminal procedure provides that the king may issue a pardon "on pardonable matters" for public crimes only. Such pardons are generally issued annually during the holy month of Ramadan, in advance of which the Ministry of Interior publishes a list of terms and conditions defining eligibility to receive a royal pardon (see also section 1.d.). The stated conditions generally exclude specific criminal categories, for example, those convicted of crimes involving state security. The law of criminal procedure states that a victim's heirs may grant a pardon for private crimes.

On January 2, authorities executed 47 individuals. Among them was prominent Shia cleric and political activist Nimr al-Nimr, who was charged with inciting terrorism and sedition, interfering in the affairs of another country, disobeying the country's guardians, attacking security personnel during his arrest, and meeting with wanted criminals. International human rights organizations claimed al-Nimr was executed because of his sermons criticizing authorities and calling attention to discrimination against Saudi Shia. Local and international human rights organizations noted that his trial before the Specialized Criminal Court (SCC) lacked transparency and did not adhere to minimum fair trial standards.

On December 6, the SCC handed down initial death sentences to 15 individuals and sentenced 15 others to prison terms for spying for Iran; two additional individuals were acquitted. As of year's end, the sentences were under appeal. HRW issued a report in May that claimed there were multiple due process violations in the trials of the men, many of whom were reportedly Shia. HRW further claimed that they had been held incommunicado in pretrial detention for a prolonged period without access to legal counsel and that, before and throughout court proceedings, their legal counsel was not able to review the evidence against them.

The government also imposes death sentences for crimes committed by minors. According to accounts from local and international human rights organizations, family members, and local media, at least three individuals executed on January 2--Mustafa Abkar, Ali al-Ribh, and Amin al-Ghamidi--may have been minors when they allegedly committed the crimes for which they were convicted.

On July 27, the SCC in Riyadh sentenced Abdulkareem al-Hawaj to death for crimes he allegedly committed in 2012 at age 16, including "throwing two Molotov cocktails," "participating in riots that resulted in the shooting of an armored vehicle," "participating in illegal gatherings," "chanting against the state," and using social media "to insult the leaders," according to a September 9 Amnesty International report. As of year's end, the sentence was under appeal.

In September 2015 the Supreme Court affirmed the 2014 death sentence for Ali Mohammed Baqir al-Nimr, the nephew of Nimr al-Nimr, who was convicted of crimes he allegedly committed when he was 17. Al-Nimr was charged with protesting, making, and throwing Molotov cocktails at police, aiding and abetting fugitives, attempting to attack security vehicles, encouraging others to participate in protests, and involvement with individuals who possessed and distributed ammunition, according to some media sources whose accuracy could not be verified. Human rights organizations reported due process concerns relating to minimum fair trial standards, including allegations that authorities arrested al-Nimr without a warrant, obtained a confession using torture, and repeatedly denied him access to his lawyer during the sentencing and appeals process. In September and October 2015, the Supreme Court upheld death sentences for Dawood al-Marhoon and Abdullah al-Zaher, convicted of crimes allegedly committed when they were 17 and 15, respectively. As of year's end, these executions had not been carried out.

Executions were sometimes conducted for nonviolent offenses. HRW reported that as of July 27, authorities had executed 13 persons for nonviolent crimes related to drug smuggling.

Suicide bombers conducted a number of attacks throughout the year, killing both civilians and government security forces; Da'esh claimed responsibility for some of those attacks. A January 29 attack on a Shia mosque in al-Ahsa left five dead and 18 wounded. An April 28 attack on a police station, also in al-Ahsa, injured one police officer. On July 4, suicide bombers conducted apparently coordinated attacks in Medina, Qatif, and Jeddah. In Medina a suicide bomber detonated an explosives belt outside of the Prophet's mosque, killing four persons and wounding five. In Qatif three suicide bombers detonated explosives belts outside a mosque but did not harm anyone else in the incident. In Jeddah a suicide bomber detonated an explosives belt near a foreign consulate in Jeddah, injuring two police officers.

b. Disappearance

There were no reports of politically motivated disappearances (for information on detentions without prompt notification of charges or release, see section 1.d.).

c. Torture and Other Cruel, Inhuman, or Degrading Treatment or Punishment

The law prohibits torture and holds criminal investigation officers accountable for any abuse of authority. Sharia, as interpreted in the country, prohibits judges from accepting confessions obtained under duress. Statutory law provides that public investigators shall not subject accused persons to coercive measures to influence their testimony.

There were no confirmed reports of torture by government officials during the year, but numerous prisoners were serving sentences based on confessions they claimed were obtained through torture or mistreatment. Amnesty International, HRW, and other human rights organizations reported cases in which the SCC based its decisions on confessions allegedly obtained through torture and admitted as evidence. The UN Committee against Torture also noted that courts admitted coerced confessions as evidence. According to the committee, SCC judges "repeatedly refused to act on claims made by defendants facing terrorism charges that they were subjected to torture or ill-treatment during interrogations for the purpose of compelling a confession, including in the cases of Fadhel al-Manasif, Ali al-Nimr, Dawoud al-Marhoun, and Abdullah al-Zaher" (see section 1.a.). In 2015 the Supreme Court upheld death sentences for al-Nimr, al-Marhoon, and al-Zaher (see section 1.a.), as well as other Shia activists who claimed that authorities tortured them to obtain confessions. Amnesty International reported that Ali al-Nimr said authorities obtained his confession under torture during interrogation sessions held during six months of pretrial detention in 2012.

The UN committee also reported that complaints of torture and mistreatment by members of the Commission for the Promotion of Virtue and Prevention of Vice (CPVPV) were rarely investigated, creating a climate of impunity. On April 10, the cabinet (or Council of Ministers) issued a decree stripping the CPVPV of authority to pursue suspects, ask for their identification, and arrest or detain them.

Former detainees in facilities run by the General Investigations Directorate (the country's internal security forces, also known as "Mabahith") alleged that abuse included sleep deprivation or long periods of solitary confinement for nonviolent detainees. Former detainees in Mabahith-run al-Ha'ir Prison claimed that, while physical abuse was uncommon in detention, Mabahith officials sometimes resorted to mental or psychological abuse of detainees, particularly during the interrogation phase. Ministry of Interior officials claimed that rules prohibiting torture prevented such practices from occurring in the penal system. The ministry installed surveillance cameras to record interrogations of suspects in criminal investigation offices, some police stations, and in prisons where such interrogations regularly occurred, such as the ministry's General Investigations Directorate/Mabahith prison facilities.

Representatives from the governmental Human Rights Commission (HRC) and the quasi-governmental National Society for Human Rights (NSHR), supported by a trust funded by the estate of the late King Fahd, conducted prison visits to ascertain whether torture occurred in prisons or detention centers and maintained permanent branches in eight facilities. Independent institutions did not conduct regular, unannounced visits to places of detention, according to the UN Committee against Torture.

The courts continued to use corporal punishment as a judicial penalty, usually in the form of floggings, whippings, or lashings, a common punishment that government officials defended as dictated by sharia. According to local human rights activists, police conducted the floggings according to a set of guidelines determined by local interpretation of sharia. The police official administering the punishment must place a copy of the Quran under his arm that prevents raising the hand above the head, limiting the ability to inflict pain on the person subjected to the punishment, and instructions forbid police from breaking the skin or causing scarring when administering the lashes.

In February a Saudi appeals court returned a death sentence from the Abha General Court for Ashraf Fayadh, a Saudi resident of Palestinian origin, whom the court had found guilty of apostasy, spreading atheism, threatening the morals of Saudi society, and having illicit relations with women. He was sentenced to death for apostasy because of poetry he wrote was deemed offensive to Islam. The lower court then commuted his death sentence to an eight-year prison term and 800 lashes while maintaining the guilty verdict.

In February the Medina Criminal Court reportedly sentenced a 28-year-old man to 10 years in prison and 2,000 lashes for expressing his atheism on Twitter, according to the local newspaper *al-Watan*.

There were no reported cases of judicially administered amputation during the year.

Prison and Detention Center Conditions

Prison and detention center conditions varied, and some did not meet international standards.

<u>Physical Conditions</u>: Juveniles constituted fewer than 1 percent of detainees and were held in separate facilities from adults, according to available information. Although information on the maximum capacity of the facilities was not available, overcrowding in some detention centers was reported to be a problem. Violations listed in NSHR reports following prison visits documented shortages of and improperly trained wardens and lack of prompt access to medical treatment when requested. Some detained individuals complained about lack of access to adequate health-care services, including medication. Some prisoners alleged that prison authorities maintained cold temperatures in prison facilities and deliberately kept lights on 24 hours a day to make prisoners uncomfortable.

Human rights activists reported that deaths in prisons, jails, or pretrial detention centers were infrequent. In May local media reported that two female inmates died at a rehabilitation center at the Malaz Prison, but the circumstances of their death were unclear.

Authorities held pretrial detainees together with convicted prisoners. They separated persons suspected or convicted of terrorism offenses from the general population but held them in similar facilities. Activists alleged that authorities sometimes detained individuals in the same cells as individuals with mental disabilities as a form of punishment and indicated that authorities mistreated persons with disabilities.

<u>Administration</u>: There were multiple legal authorities for prisons and detention centers. Local provincial authorities administered approximately 90 local jails, and the Ministry of Interior administered approximately 20 regional prisons and detention centers. Recordkeeping on prisoners was inadequate; there were reports authorities held prisoners after they had completed their sentences. A Ministry of Interior-run website provided detainees and their relatives access to a database containing information about the legal status of the detainee, including any scheduled trial dates.

Authorities differentiated between violent and nonviolent prisoners, sometimes pardoning nonviolent prisoners to reduce the prison population. Certain prisoners convicted on terrorism-related charges were required to participate in government-sponsored rehabilitation programs before being considered for release.

No ombudsmen were available to register or investigate complaints made by prisoners, although prisoners could and did submit complaints to the HRC and the NSHR for investigation. There was no information available on whether prisoners were able to submit complaints to judicial authorities without censorship or whether authorities investigated credible allegations of inhuman conditions and treatment and made them public.

Authorities generally permitted relatives and friends to visit prisoners twice a week, although certain prisons limited visitation to once every 15 days, and there were reports that prison officials denied this privilege in some instances. The families of detainees could access a website for the Ministry of Interior's General Directorate of Prisons that contained forms to apply for prison visits, temporary leave from prison (generally approved around the post-Ramadan Eid holidays), and release on bail (for pretrial detainees). Family members of detained persons complained that authorities canceled scheduled visits with their relatives without reason.

Authorities permitted Muslim detainees and prisoners to perform religious observances such as prayers, but prison authorities in Mabahith prison facilities reportedly did not arrange for detainees to conduct Friday Islamic congregational prayer services.

HRW reported that activist Khalid al-Umair remained in prison following the completion of his eight-year sentence on October 5. Al-Umair was arrested in 2009 for attempting to protest against Israel's military operations in Gaza. A Gulf-based NGO reported that, as of November 3, al-Umair was transferred from al-Ha'ir Prison to Mohammed bin Nayef Counseling and Care Center in preparation for his release; he remained there at year's end.

Independent Monitoring: No independent human rights observers visited prisons or detention centers during the year. The government permitted foreign diplomats to visit prison facilities to view general conditions in nonconsular cases. In a limited number of cases, foreign diplomats visited individuals in detention, but the visits took place in a separate visitors' center where conditions may have differed from those in the detention facilities holding the prisoners. The most recent prison visit conducted by an independent human rights organization was a 2006 visit by HRW. In August security officials stated they permitted foreign journalists to visit a security prison in Jeddah during the year. The government permitted the governmental HRC and domestic quasi-governmental organizations, such as the NSHR, to monitor prison conditions. The organizations stated they visited prisons throughout the country and reported on prison conditions. The NSHR monitored health care in prisons and brought deficiencies to the attention of the Ministry of Interior. In 2015 the NSHR documented 422 prison-related complaints, including lack of access to medical care, poor hygiene and sanitation, overcrowding, poor ventilation, and understaffing.

d. Arbitrary Arrest or Detention

The law provides that no entity may restrict a person's actions or imprison a person, except under provisions of the law. The law of criminal procedure provides that authorities may not detain a person for more than 24 hours, except pursuant to a written order from a public investigator. Authorities must inform the detained person of the reasons for detention. Regardless, the Ministry of Interior, to which the majority of forces with arrest powers reported, maintained broad authority in law and in practice to arrest and detain persons indefinitely without judicial oversight, notification of charges against them, or effective access to legal counsel or family. Authorities held persons for months and sometimes years without charge or trial and reportedly failed to advise them promptly of their rights, including their legal right to be represented by an attorney. Under the law detentions can be extended administratively for up to six months at the discretion of the Bureau of Investigation and Public Prosecution.

The 2014 counterterrorism law provides that an investigatory body may detain an individual accused of any crime under that law for a period of six months and may extend the detention an additional six months. By law, defendants accused of any crime cited in the law are entitled to hire a practicing lawyer to defend themselves before the court "within an adequate period of time to be decided by the investigatory body."

Role of the Police and Security Apparatus

The king and the Ministries of Defense and Interior, in addition to the Ministry of National Guard, are responsible for law enforcement and maintenance of order. The Ministry of Interior exercises primary control over internal security and police forces. The civil police and the internal security police have authority to arrest and detain individuals. Military and security courts investigated abuses of authority and security force killings. Civilian authorities maintained effective control over security forces, and the government had mechanisms to investigate and punish abuse and corruption. There were no confirmed reports of impunity involving the security forces during the year, although the UN Committee against Torture noted that the lack of frequent investigations into abuses created a climate of impunity (see section 1.c.).

The CPVPV, which monitors public behavior to enforce strict adherence to the official interpretation of Islamic norms, reports to the king via the Royal Diwan (royal court) and to the Ministry of Interior. In 2015 the CPVPV had 533 offices throughout the kingdom. In April the cabinet issued regulations severely curtailing the CPVPV's enforcement powers. The new regulations prohibit CPVPV officers from investigating, detaining or arresting, or requesting the identification of any individual and limit their activities to providing counseling and reporting individuals suspected of violating the law to police or other authorities. Evidence available at year's end indicated that CPVPV officers were less visibly present and active after implementation of the new strictures.

Ministry of Interior police and security forces were generally effective at maintaining law and order. The Board of Grievances ("Diwan al-Mazalim"), a high-level administrative judicial body that specializes in cases against government entities and reports directly to the king, is the only formal mechanism available to seek redress for claims of abuse. Citizens may report abuses by security forces at any police station, to the HRC, or to the NSHR. The HRC and NSHR maintained records of complaints and outcomes, but privacy laws protected information about individual cases, and information was not publicly available. During the year the Board of Grievances held hearings and adjudicated claims of wrongdoing, but there were no reported prosecutions of security force members for human rights violations. The HRC, in cooperation with the Ministry of Education, provided materials and training to police, security forces, and the CPVPV on protecting human rights.

Officers of the Mabahith also have broad authorities to investigate, detain, and forward to judicial authorities "national security" cases--which ranged from terrorism cases to dissident and human rights activist cases--separate from the Bureau of Investigation and Public Prosecution (BIPP). A 2014 Ministry of Justice decree formalized and reaffirmed the role of the SCC, founded in 2008 to try terrorism offenses, following the promulgation of a counterterrorism law that year.

The BIPP and the Control and Investigation Board are the two units of the government with authority to investigate reports of criminal activity, corruption, and "disciplinary cases" involving government employees. These bodies are responsible for investigating potential cases and referring them to the administrative courts. Legal authorities for investigation and public prosecution of criminal offenses are consolidated within the BIPP; the Control and Investigation Board is responsible for investigation and prosecution of noncriminal cases. All financial audit and control functions are limited to the General Auditing Board.

Arrest Procedures and Treatment of Detainees

According to the law of criminal procedure, "no person shall be arrested, searched, detained, or imprisoned except in cases provided by law, and any accused person shall have the right to seek the assistance of a lawyer or a representative to defend him during the investigation and trial stages." By law, authorities may summon any person for investigation and may issue an arrest warrant based on evidence. In practice, however, authorities frequently did not use warrants, and warrants were not required in cases where probable cause existed.

The law requires that authorities file charges within 72 hours of arrest and hold a trial within six months, subject to exceptions specified by amendments to the law of criminal procedure and the counterterrorism law (see section 2.a.). Authorities may not legally detain a person under arrest for more than 24 hours, except pursuant to a written order from a public investigator. Authorities reportedly often failed to observe these legal protections, and there was no requirement to advise suspects of their rights. Judicial proceedings began after authorities completed a full investigation, which in some cases took years.

The law of criminal procedure specifies procedures required for extending the detention period of an accused person beyond the initial five days. As amended by royal decree in 2013, the law expands the number of individuals empowered to renew pretrial detentions for periods of up to six months to include the president of the BIPP and designated subordinates. The amended text allows authorities to approve official detentions in excess of six months in "exceptional circumstances," effectively allowing individuals to be held in pretrial detention indefinitely. Another amendment extends from three months to six months the deadline for the BIPP to gather evidence against the accused and issue a warrant for the defendant's arrest, summons, or detention. This provision is also contained in the counterterrorism law, subject to the approval of the extension by the SCC. Another amendment explicitly allows an individual to represent himself in court.

There is a functioning bail system for less serious criminal charges. Detainees generally did not have the right to obtain a lawyer of their choice. In normal cases the government typically provided lawyers to defendants, although defendants must make a formal application to the Ministry of Justice to receive a court-appointed lawyer and prove their inability to pay for their legal representation. Human rights activists often did not trust the courts to appoint lawyers for them due to concern the lawyer would be biased. The law contains no provision for the right to be informed of the protections guaranteed under the law.

Incommunicado detention was sometimes a problem. Authorities reportedly did not always respect a detainees' right to contact family members following arrest, and the counterterrorism law allows the Ministry of Interior to hold a defendant for up to 90 days in detention without access to family members or legal counsel. Security and some other types of prisoners sometimes remained in detention for long periods before family members or associates received information of their whereabouts, particularly for detainees in Mabahith-run facilities.

Arbitrary Arrest: There were reports of arbitrary arrest and detention. During the year authorities detained without charge security suspects, persons who publicly criticized the government, Shia religious leaders, and persons who violated religious standards. Saleh al-Ashwan, a member of the Saudi Association for Political and Civil Rights (ACPRA), was detained in 2012 and held without charge until 2016, when the SCC sentenced him to five years in prison and a five-year travel ban, according to human rights organizations. In November the UN Working Group on Arbitrary Detention renewed its call "for the immediate release of [nine] detainees and the provision of reparations for the harm caused" on the anniversary of the expert panel's formal opinion that the detentions of human rights activists Sulaiman al-Rashudi, Abdullah al-Hamid, Mohammed al-Qahtani, Abdulkareem Yousef al-Khoder, Mohammed Saleh al-Bajadi, Omar al-Hamid al-Sa'id, Raif Badawi, Fadhel al-Manasif, and Waleed Abu al-Khair were arbitrary. The statement also called for "other [unnamed] prisoners being held in similar circumstances" to be freed.

Pretrial Detention: Lengthy pretrial detention was a problem. In the past local unlicensed NGOs, such as ACPRA and the Adala Center for Human Rights, challenged the Ministry of Interior publicly and in court on cases considered to involve arbitrary arrest or detention. The two NGOs ceased operating in 2013 and 2014, respectively, after authorities ordered them disbanded. ACPRA claimed the ministry sometimes ignored judges' rulings (see section 2.b.).

There was no information available on the percentage of the prison population in pretrial detention or the average length of time held. Local human rights activists knew of dozens of cases and reportedly received regular reports from families claiming authorities held their relatives arbitrarily or without notification of charges.

During the year the Ministry of Interior stated it had detained numerous individuals for terrorist acts. On September 29, local media reported there were 5,277 terror suspects detained by the Ministry of Interior in public security prisons.

Detainee's Ability to Challenge Lawfulness of Detention before a Court: Detainees are not entitled under the law to challenge the lawfulness of their detention before a court. In the case of wrongful detention, the law of criminal procedure, as well as provisions of the counterterrorism law, provide for the right to compensation if detainees are found to have been held unlawfully.

Amnesty: The king continued the tradition of commuting some judicial punishments. Royal pardons sometimes set aside a conviction and sometimes reduced or eliminated corporal punishment. The remaining sentence could be added to a new sentence if the pardoned prisoner committed a crime subsequent to release.

Authorities did not detain some individuals who had received prison sentences. The counterterrorism law allows the interior minister to stop proceedings against an individual who cooperates with investigations or helps thwart a planned terrorist attack. The minister may also release individuals already convicted on such charges.

e. Denial of Fair Public Trial

The law provides that judges are independent and not subject to any authority other than the provisions of sharia and the laws in force. Nevertheless, the judiciary was not independent, as it was required to coordinate its decisions with executive authorities, with the king as final arbiter. Although public allegations of interference with judicial independence were rare, the judiciary reportedly was subject to influence, particularly in the case of legal decisions rendered by specialized judicial bodies, such as the SCC, which rarely acquitted suspects. Human rights activists reported that SCC judges received implicit instructions to issue harsh sentences against human rights activists, reformers, journalists, and dissidents not engaged in violent activities.

There were some reports during the year of courts exercising jurisdiction over senior members of the royal family. In October multiple media reported that Prince Turki bin Saud al-Kabir, a member of the royal family, was executed after having been found guilty of murder. In November, the *Okaz* newspaper reported that an unidentified prince was lashed in a Jeddah prison as part of a court-ordered sentence that also included time in prison.

Trial Procedures

In the judicial system, there is no case law (in the form of published judicial opinions), no uniform criminal code, and no doctrine of stare decisis that binds judges to follow a legal precedent. The law states that defendants should be treated equally in accordance with sharia. The Council of Senior Scholars (CSS), or the "ulema", an autonomous advisory body, issues religious opinions (fatwas) that guide how judges interpret sharia.

In the absence of a penal code detailing all criminal offenses and punishments, judges in the courts determine many of these penalties through their interpretations of sharia, which varied according to the judge and the circumstances of the case. Because judges have considerable discretion in decision making, rulings and sentences diverged widely from case to case. Several laws passed in the last decade, however, provide sentencing requirements for crimes including terrorism, cybercrimes, trafficking in persons, and domestic abuse. In December the Ministry of Justice completed a compilation of previous decisions that judges could refer to as a point of reference in making rulings and assigning sentences.

According to judicial procedures, appeals courts cannot independently reverse lower court judgments; they are limited to affirming judgments or returning them to a lower court for modification. Even when judges did not affirm judgments, appeals judges in some cases remanded the judgment to the judge who originally authored the opinion. This procedure sometimes made it difficult for parties to receive a ruling that differed from the original judgment in cases where judges hesitated to admit error. While judges may base their decisions on any of the four Sunni schools of jurisprudence, all of which are represented in the CSS, the Hanbali school predominates and forms the basis for the country's law and legal interpretations of sharia. Shia citizens use their legal traditions to adjudicate family law cases between Shia parties, although either party can decide to adjudicate a case in state courts, which use Sunni legal tradition.

According to the law, there is no presumption of innocence. While the law states that court hearings shall be public, courts may be closed at the judge's discretion. As a result, many trials during the year were closed. Foreign diplomatic missions were able to obtain permission to attend nonconsular court proceedings (that is, cases to which neither the host country nor any of its nationals were a party; diplomatic missions are generally allowed to attend consular proceedings of their own nationals), and they did so throughout the year. To attend, authorities required diplomats to obtain advance written approval from the Ministry of Foreign Affairs, the Ministry of Justice, the court administration, and the presiding judge. Authorities sometimes did not permit entry to such trials to individuals other than diplomats who were not the legal agents or family members of the accused. SCC officials sometimes prevented individuals from attending trial sessions for seemingly trivial reasons, such as banning female relatives or diplomats from attending due to the absence of women officers to inspect the women upon entry to the courtroom. According to the Ministry of Justice, authorities may close a trial depending on the sensitivity of the case to national security, the reputation of the defendant, or the safety of witnesses.

Representatives of the HRC, the Ministry of Justice, and sometimes representatives of the media regularly attended trials at the SCC.

Amendments to the law of criminal procedure in 2013 strengthened provisions stating that authorities will offer defendants a lawyer at government expense. Human rights activists, however, reported that the process for applying for a court-appointed lawyer was difficult and cumbersome, and many said they did not trust the process due to concern that the lawyer would be biased.

The law provides defendants the right to be present at trial and to consult with an attorney during the investigation and trial. The counterterrorism law, however, limits the right of defendants accused of terrorism to access legal representation while under investigation and provides for that access only after an unspecified period of time, "before the matter goes to court within a timeframe determined by the investigative entity." There is no right to discovery or inspection of government-held evidence, nor can defendants view their own file, the minutes from their interrogation, or all of the evidence against them. Defendants may request to review evidence, but the court decides whether to grant the request. Defendants also have the right to call and cross-examine witnesses. The law provides that a BIPP-appointed investigator questions the witnesses called by the defendant during the investigation phase before the initiation of a trial and may hear testimony of additional witnesses he deems necessary to determine the facts.

Authorities may not subject a defendant to any coercive measures or compel the taking of an oath. The court must inform convicted persons of their right to appeal rulings.

The law does not provide for free interpretation services. The law of criminal procedure provides only that "the court should seek the assistance of interpreters," but it does not obligate the court to do so from the moment the defendant is charged, nor does the law specify that the state will bear the costs of such services.

While sharia as interpreted by the government applies to all citizens and noncitizens, the law and practice discriminate against women, noncitizens, nonpracticing Sunni, Shia, and persons of other religions. For example, in most cases a woman's testimony before a court counts as only half that of a man's. Judges may discount the testimony of nonpracticing Sunni Muslims, Shia Muslims, or persons of other religions; sources reported that judges sometimes completely disregarded or refused to hear testimony by Shia.

Among many reports of abuses or violations of due process rights was that of Mohammed Saleh al-Bajady, a political dissident and founding member of ACPRA. Authorities originally arrested al-Bajady in 2011 for his leadership role in ACPRA and for publicly demanding political and legal reforms, including calls for a constitutional monarchy in the kingdom and protection for freedom of expression and association. During al-Bajady's trial, the court denied observers access to hearings and refused to allow his lawyer access to the courtroom. In 2012 authorities sentenced him to four years' imprisonment and a subsequent five-year international travel ban. He was released in 2013, but a week later, authorities reincarcerated him. In 2014 authorities announced they would retry al-Bajady before the SCC in relation to his human rights activities. In March 2015 the SCC sentenced al-Bajady to 10 years in prison; a court of appeals reportedly reduced the sentence to eight years, with four years suspended and including time served. In November 2015 al-Bajady was released from prison to a rehabilitation program, then to a Ministry of Interior "rest house," and fully released on April 7, but with a travel ban until 2020.

On September 5, the SCC sentenced one of ACPRA's members, Omar al-Sa'id, to seven years in prison, followed by a 10-year travel ban, on charges for which he had reportedly already been tried, convicted, and served time. In 2013 authorities detained al-Sa'id and the Buraydah Criminal Court initially sentenced him to 300 lashes and four years in prison for calling for a constitutional monarchy and criticizing the country's human rights record. The case was returned on appeal to the issuing court and then transferred to the SCC, which ruled in November 2015 to reduce his sentence to two and one-half years, including time already served. He was released in December 2015 upon completion of the sentence. Following his release, the case was reopened, and the SCC subsequently issued the September 5 ruling that increased his sentence from two and one-half to seven years in prison; al-Said remained in detention at year's end.

In 2014 authorities retried human rights lawyer Waleed Abu al-Khair before the SCC, and the court handed down a 15-year sentence, with a subsequent 15-year international travel ban after his release and a fine of 200,000 riyals ($53,300), upheld on appeal in January 2015. Previously, the Jeddah Criminal Court sentenced him to a three-month prison term on a virtually identical set of charges, all of which related to his human rights work, public calls for reform, criticisms of government policies and officials, and his role in founding an unlicensed NGO, the Monitor for Human Rights in Saudi Arabia.

Political Prisoners and Detainees

The number of political prisoners, including detainees who reportedly remained in prolonged detention without charge, could not be reliably ascertained.

In many cases it was impossible to determine the legal basis for incarceration and whether the detention complied with international norms and standards. Those who remained imprisoned after trial, including persons who were political activists openly critical of the government, were often convicted of terrorism-related crimes, and there was not sufficient public information about the alleged crimes to judge whether they had a credible claim to being political prisoners. The SCC tried political and human rights activists each year for actions unrelated to terrorism or violence against the state.

International NGOs criticized the government for abusing its antiterrorism prerogatives to arrest some members of the political opposition who had not espoused or committed violence and detain them on security-related grounds. High-profile prisoners were generally treated well. Authorities sometimes restricted legal access to detainees; no international humanitarian organizations had access to them.

On December 1, an SCC appellate court increased the initial sentence issued on April 24 for Eissa al-Hamid, a cofounder of ACPRA, from nine to 11 years in prison, followed by a travel ban of 11 years, and levied a fine of 100,000 riyals

($27,000) against him on charges that included "communicating false information to undermine the image of the state," according to the Agence France-Presse. On May 29, the SCC sentenced ACPRA founding-member Abdulaziz al-Shobaily to eight years in prison, followed by an eight-year travel ban, on charges related to his membership in a human rights organization. On November 3, local media reported that the SCC in Qatif sentenced a citizen to 10 years' imprisonment and a 50,000 riyals ($13,300) fine for joining ACPRA and sentenced another to 15 years' imprisonment for sympathizing with Nimr al-Nimr and calling for demonstrations against the government.

In January 2015 authorities administered 50 lashes to Raif Badawi, a nonviolent activist and blogger sentenced to 10 years in prison and 1,000 lashes in 2014 on charges related to insulting Islam (see section 2.a.). As of year's end, Badawi remained in Burayman Prison in Jeddah; authorities had not yet carried out the remainder of the lashing sentence.

In 2014 the SCC sentenced Shia activist Fadhel al-Manasif to 15 years in prison and a 15-year travel ban for breaking allegiance with the king and harming the country's reputation, among other charges, according to media and NGO reporting.

Civil Judicial Procedures and Remedies

Complainants claiming human rights violations generally sought assistance from the HRC or the NSHR, which either advocated on their behalf or provided courts with opinions on their cases. The HRC generally responded to complaints and could refer cases to the BIPP; domestic violence cases were the most common. Individuals or organizations may petition directly for damages or government action to end human rights violations before the Board of Grievances, except in compensation cases related to state security where the SCC handles remediation. The counterterrorism law contains a provision allowing detainees in Mabahith-run prisons to request financial compensation from the Ministry of Interior for wrongful detention beyond their prison terms.

In some cases the government did not carry out judicially ordered compensation for unlawful detentions in a timely manner.

f. Arbitrary or Unlawful Interference with Privacy, Family, Home, or Correspondence

The law prohibits unlawful intrusions into the privacy of persons, their homes, places of work, and vehicles. Criminal investigation officers are required to maintain records of all searches conducted; these records should contain the name of the officer conducting the search, the text of the search warrant (or an explanation of the urgency that necessitated the search without a warrant), and the names and signatures of the persons who were present at the time of search. While the law also provides for the privacy of all mail, telegrams, telephone conversations, and other means of communication, the government did not respect the privacy of correspondence or communications and used the considerable latitude provided by law to monitor activities legally and intervene where it deemed necessary.

There were reports from human rights activists of governmental monitoring or blocking mobile telephone or internet usage before planned demonstrations. The government strictly monitored politically related activities and took punitive actions, including arrest and detention, against persons engaged in certain political activities, such as direct public criticism of senior members of the royal family by name, forming a political party, or organizing a demonstration. Customs officials reportedly routinely opened mail and shipments to search for contraband. In some areas Ministry of Interior informants allegedly reported "seditious ideas," "antigovernment activity," or "behavior contrary to Islam" in their neighborhoods.

The counterterrorism law allows the Ministry of Interior to access a terrorism suspect's private communications as well as banking information in a manner inconsistent with the legal protections provided by criminal procedure law.

The CPVPV monitored and regulated public interaction between members of the opposite sex. In May local media reported that police, acting on information from the CPVPV, arrested one unrelated couple for traveling together in the same car and another unrelated couple for traveling together on a motorcycle.

g. Abuses in Internal Conflict

In March 2015, in response to a request from Yemeni president Abd Rabbuh Mansour Hadi for Arab League/Gulf Cooperation Council military intervention, Saudi officials announced the formation of a coalition to counter the 2014 overthrow of the legitimate government in Yemen by militias of the Ansar Allah movement (also known colloquially as "Houthis") and forces loyal to former Yemeni president Ali Abdullah Saleh. Membership in the coalition included the United Arab Emirates, Bahrain, Egypt, Jordan, Kuwait, Morocco, Qatar, Somalia,

Sudan, and Senegal. The Saudi-led coalition conducted air and ground operations throughout 2015 and, to a more limited extent, between the months of April and August, as a result of a cease-fire agreement that limited air and ground operations during peace talks held in Kuwait. Following the suspension of the talks in August, the coalition resumed military operations.

Killings: NGOs, media, and humanitarian and international organizations reported on what they characterized as disproportionate and indiscriminate use of force by all parties to the conflict in Yemen, including the Saudi-led coalition.

Coalition airstrikes resulted in civilian casualties and damage to infrastructure on multiple occasions. For example, an airstrike on a funeral hall in Sanaa, Yemen, on October 8 killed at least 140 persons and wounded more than 500, including children, according to international media reports.

The UN high commissioner for human rights stated that between March 2015 and August 23, an estimated 3,799 civilians had been killed and 6,711 injured as result of the war in Yemen. His office released a report containing examples of possible violations of international humanitarian law and international human rights law by the coalition that had occurred through June, including those involving airstrikes on residential areas, marketplaces, and medical and educational facilities. On March 15, for example, coalition airstrikes allegedly killed 107 civilians, injured 37 civilians, and destroyed 16 shops in a market in Mustaba district of Hajjah Governorate.

The coalition's Joint Incident Assessment Team (JIAT), established by the government, based in Riyadh, and consisting of military and civilian members from coalition member states, investigated some incidents of airstrikes that reportedly resulted in civilian casualties as well as claims by international organizations that humanitarian aid convoys and infrastructure were targeted by the coalition. On December 7, the JIAT released summaries of reports of five incidents, including the August 15 attack against a Doctors without Borders (MSF) facility in the Abs district of Hajjah Governorate. In August the JIAT released a press statement with summary findings of eight such investigations. The JIAT also issued a press statement on its initial investigation of the October 8 funeral hall airstrike, claiming that a Yemeni party passed the coalition information that inaccurately reported the funeral hall was a military target and recommending that action be taken against those who caused the incident. It recommended that the coalition review its rules of engagement and that families of the victims receive compensation. In addition, the JIAT recommended in two separate incidents an investigation into potential violations of the rules of engagement and accountability for those involved in two other incidents. The JIAT was established by the government to identify lessons and corrective actions and to cue national accountability mechanisms, as appropriate. The JIAT's investigations had not led to any prosecutions as of year's end.

Houthi militias and forces allied with former president Saleh fired long-range missiles into or towards Saudi Arabia nearly 30 times between January 1 and December 31, according to the Center for Strategic and International Studies and media reports. Saudi media reported more than 40,000 projectiles had been launched into Saudi territory from Yemen since March 2015, destroying hospitals, schools, homes, and other infrastructure. In August media reported that authorities in Najran said Houthi-Saleh militias had partially or totally destroyed 1,074 homes and 108 commercial establishments since March 2015. More than 370 Saudi civilians were killed along the Saudi southern border in the same period, according to Saudi media reports.

Other Conflict-related Abuse: There were reports of restrictions on the free passage of relief supplies and of humanitarian organizations' access to those individuals most in need, perpetrated by all sides in the conflict, including the Saudi-led coalition. Some media reported the Yemen government and/or the coalition delayed or denied clearance permits for humanitarian and commercial aid shipments bound for rebel-held Red Sea ports. Other sources reported the Houthi-Saleh militias' forceful takeover and misadministration of Yemen government institutions led to dire economic consequences--the nonpayment of workers' wages, unmaintained and unrepaired gantry cranes at ports where aid materiel was offloaded, and allegations of widespread corruption, including at checkpoints controlled by Houthi-Saleh militias--which severely impacted the distribution of food aid and exacerbated food insecurity.

According to an HRW report published in July, coalition airstrikes damaged many factories and structures used for humanitarian and economic purposes during the year. HRW reported that: an airstrike on January 6 damaged a hangar containing food products including rice and sugar at Hudaydah Port; on February 2 and 5, two airstrikes on a cement factory in Amran killed 15 civilians and damaged buildings around the factory; and on August 11 and 12, airstrikes destroyed Aldarejh Bridge, used by the World Food Program to transport approximately 90 percent of its food deliveries for the northern governorates, forcing it to use alternate supply routes. As a result of the conflict, the humanitarian situation in the country deteriorated significantly, with 14.1 million food insecure people and a reported 69 percent of the country's population requiring humanitarian assistance by the end of the year, according to the UN.

On August 15, a coalition airstrike destroyed an MSF hospital in Hajjah Governorate, which MSF stated killed 19 persons, including one MSF staff member, and injured 24. Later that month MSF announced that it would evacuate its staff from six hospitals in northern Yemen because it could not receive assurances that its hospitals would not be bombed again.

For additional details, including additional information on the Saudi-led coalition's operations in Yemen, see the Department of State's *Country Reports on Human Rights* for Yemen.

Section 2. Respect for Civil Liberties, Including:

a. Freedom of Speech and Press

Civil law does not protect human rights, including freedoms of speech and of the press; only local interpretation and the practice of sharia protect these rights. There were frequent reports of restrictions on free speech. The Basic Law specifies, "Mass media and all other vehicles of expression shall employ civil and polite language, contribute towards the education of the nation, and strengthen unity. The media are prohibited from committing acts that lead to disorder and division, affect the security of the state or its public relations, or undermine human dignity and rights." Authorities are responsible for regulating and determining which speech or expression undermines internal security. The government can ban or suspend media outlets if it concludes they violated the press and publications law, and it monitored and blocked hundreds of thousands of internet sites.

The legal definition of terrorism, according to the counterterrorism law, includes "any act…intended to disturb the public order of the state…or insult the reputation of the state or its position." Local human rights activists and international human rights organizations criticized the law for its vague definition of terrorism and complained the government could use it to prosecute peaceful dissidents for "insulting the state."

Freedom of Speech and Expression: The government monitored public expressions of opinion and took advantage of legal controls to impede the free expression of opinion and restrict individuals from engaging in public criticism of the political sphere. The law forbids apostasy and blasphemy, which legally can carry the death penalty, although there were no recent instances of death sentences being carried out for these crimes (see section 1.a.). Statements that authorities construed as constituting defamation of the king, the monarchy, the governing system, or the Al Saud family resulted in criminal charges for citizens advocating government reform. The government prohibits public employees from directly or indirectly engaging in dialogue with local or foreign media or participating in any meetings intended to oppose state policies.

The government charged a number of individuals with crimes related to their exercise of free speech during the year. In January local media reported that the Najran Criminal Court sentenced two Ministry of Health employees to prison terms and lashes for criticizing their hospital's administration on Twitter. On appeal, the employees were sentenced under the anticyber crimes law to prison terms of 11 months and eight months, respectively.

In February local media reported that the Medina Criminal Court sentenced a man to 10 years in prison and 2,000 lashes on charges related to "atheistic" tweets.

In September the SCC sentenced a person to seven years in prison and a travel ban of 10 years on charges of publishing rumors via Twitter, joining an unauthorized association, not pledging allegiance, calling publicly for demonstrations, and challenging the independence of the judiciary, according to local media reports.

On December 27, the media reported that a court in Dammam sentenced a man to one year in prison and a fine of 30,000 riyals ($8,000) for "incitement to end the guardianship of women" after making statements online and hanging up posters in mosques calling for an end to the male guardianship system.

Some human rights activists were detained and then released on the condition that they refrain from using social media for activism, refrain from communicating with foreign diplomats, refrain from communicating with outside human rights organizations, and refrain from traveling outside the country.

<u>Press and Media Freedoms</u>: The Press and Publications Law governs printed materials; printing presses; bookstores; the import, rental, and sale of films; television and radio; foreign media offices and their correspondents; and online newspapers and journals. The media fell under the jurisdiction of the Ministry of Culture and Information. The ministry may permanently close "whenever necessary" any means of communication--defined as any means of expressing a

viewpoint that is meant for circulation--that it deems is engaged in a prohibited activity, as set forth in the decree.

Media policy statements have urged journalists to uphold Islam, oppose atheism, promote Arab interests, and preserve cultural heritage. In 2011 a royal decree amended the press law to strengthen penalties, create a special commission to judge violations, and require all online newspapers and bloggers to obtain a license from the ministry. The decree bans publishing anything "contradicting sharia, inciting disruption, serving foreign interests that contradict national interests, and damaging the reputation of the grand mufti, members of the Council of Senior Religious Scholars, or senior government officials."

The law states that violators can face fines up to 500,000 riyals ($133,000) for each violation of the law, which is doubled if the violation is repeated. Other penalties include banning individuals from writing. While the Violations Considerations Committee in the Ministry of Culture and Information has formal responsibility for implementing the law, the Ministry of Interior, the CPVPV, and sharia court judges considered these issues regularly and exercised wide discretion in interpreting the law. It was unclear which process accords with the law.

Although satellite dishes were illegal, the government did not enforce restrictions on them, and their use was widespread. Many foreign satellite stations broadcast a wide range of programs into the country in Arabic and other languages, including foreign news channels. Access to foreign sources of information, including via satellite dishes and the internet, was common. Foreign media were subject to licensing requirements from the Ministry of Culture and Information and could not operate freely. The government filtered and at times blocked access to internet sites it considered objectionable. Privately owned satellite television networks, headquartered outside the country, maintained local offices and operated under a system of self-censorship.

<u>Violence and Harassment</u>: Authorities subjected journalists to arrests, imprisonment, and harassment during the year.

In March the SCC sentenced Eastern Province-based journalist Alaa Brinji to five years in prison and an eight-year travel ban on charges of inciting the public against the country's rulers, attempting to tarnish the country's reputation, accusing security forces of killing protesters in Awamiya, and violating the 2007 anticyber crimes law. According to human rights organizations, Brinji was arrested in 2014 and held in solitary confinement without access to a lawyer during pretrial detention.

<u>Censorship or Content Restrictions</u>: The government reportedly penalized those who published items counter to government guidelines and directly or indirectly censored the media by licensing domestic media and by controlling importation of foreign printed material. Because of self-censorship, authorities did not frequently have reason to prosecute print and broadcast media.

All newspapers in the country must be government-licensed. The Ministry of Culture and Information must approve the appointment of all senior editors and has authority to remove them. The government provided guidelines to newspapers regarding controversial issues. The Saudi Press Agency reported official government news. The government owned most print and broadcast media and book publication facilities in the country, and members of the royal family owned or influenced privately owned and nominally independent operations, including various media outlets and widely circulated pan-Arab newspapers published outside the country. Authorities prevented or delayed the distribution of foreign print media covering issues considered sensitive, effectively censoring these publications.

The government censored published material it considered blasphemous, for example, by removing works by Palestinian novelist and poet Mamoud Darwish at the Riyadh International Book Fair in 2014.

In November multiple media reported that authorities closed the al-Rawi Cultural Cafe on the campus of South Imam University in Riyadh, pending a Ministry of Culture and Information investigation into the cafe's compliance with book licensing requirements.

In some cases, however, individuals criticized specific government bodies or actions publicly without repercussions. The Consultative Council (Majlis as-Shura), an advisory body, frequently allowed print and broadcast media to observe its proceedings and meetings, but the council closed some high-profile or controversial sessions to the media.

<u>Libel/Slander Laws</u>: There were numerous reports during the year of the government using libel laws to suppress publication of material that criticized policies or public officials.

The anticyber crimes law provides for a maximum penalty of one-year's imprisonment for "defamation and infliction of damage upon others through the use of various information technology devices." In 2014 the law was amended to include social media and social networks and increases the maximum fine to 500,000 riyals ($133,000).

In June the Jeddah Criminal Court commuted a seven-year prison sentence and 2,100 lashes for an Indian man convicted of blasphemy after he converted to Islam while in prison; he was initially convicted for posting an image on Facebook of the Holy Kaaba covered with Hindu deities, according to media reports.

In February the SCC sentenced a man to 10 years in prison and a travel ban of unspecified duration for "spreading malicious rumors about the kingdom" and running a YouTube channel in which he called the country's rulers "tyrants," according to the local *Arab News* newspaper.

National Security: In most cases authorities used the anticyber crimes law and the counterterrorism law to restrict freedom of expression, including by prosecuting several individuals under these laws on charges related to statements made on social media.

Internet Freedom

The Ministry of Culture and Information or its agencies must authorize all websites registered and hosted in the country. The General Commission for Audiovisual Media has responsibility for regulating all audio and video content in the country, including satellite channels, film, music, internet, and mobile applications, independent from the Ministry of Commerce and Industry. Internet access was widely available, and more than 70 percent of the population used the internet during the year, while 83 percent had mobile broadband subscriptions, according to the Ministry of Communications and Information Technology.

The press and publications law implicitly covers electronic media, since it extends to any means of expression of a viewpoint meant for circulation, ranging from words to cartoons, photographs, and sounds. In 2011 the government issued implementing regulations for electronic publishing that set rules for internet-based and other electronic media, including chat rooms, personal blogs, and text messages. Laws, including the anticyber crimes law, criminalize defamation on the internet, hacking, unauthorized access to government websites, and stealing information related to national security as well as the creation or dissemination of a website for a terrorist organization. Security authorities actively monitored internet activity, both to enforce laws, regulations, and societal norms and to monitor recruitment efforts by extremist organizations such as Da'esh. Activists complained of monitoring or attempted monitoring of their communications on web-based communications applications. According to a 2015 Freedom House report, social media users were increasingly careful about what they posted, shared, or "liked" online, particularly after the passage of the 2014 counterterrorism law.

Access to the internet is legally available only through government-authorized internet service providers. The government required internet access providers to monitor customers and also required internet cafes to install hidden cameras and provide identity records of customers. Although authorities blocked websites offering proxies, persistent internet users accessed the unfiltered internet via other means.

On a number of occasions, government officials and senior clerics publicly warned against inaccurate reports on the internet and reminded the public that criticism of the government and its officials should be done through available private channels. The government charged those using the internet to express dissent against officials or religious authorities with terrorism, blasphemy, and apostasy.

The press and publications law criminalizes the publication or downloading of offensive sites, and authorities routinely blocked sites containing material perceived as harmful, illegal, offensive, or anti-Islamic. The governmental Communications and Information Technology Commission (CITC) filtered and blocked access to websites it deemed offensive, including adult content, as well as pages calling for domestic political, social, or economic reforms or supporting human rights, including websites of expatriate Saudi dissidents.

In October the CITC announced it blocked 2.6 million "pornographic" sites in calendar year 2015 as well 3.5 million such sites in the period from 2010 through 2015. The CITC coordinated decisions with the Saudi Arabian Monetary Agency on blocking phishing sites seeking to obtain confidential personal or financial information. Authorities submitted all other requests to block sites to an interagency committee, chaired by the Ministry of Interior, for decision. Under the Telecommunication Act, failure by service providers to block banned sites can result in a fine of five million riyals ($1.33 million).

The CITC claimed that Facebook removed materials that the CITC deemed offensive but that Twitter ignored all CITC requests. In September the CITC announced that it had not blocked any free voice, video, or messaging services after criticisms on social media that these services had been blocked. Users of Snapchat, a private messenger app, reported the CITC blocked the app during the year. Facebook Messenger and Whatsapp were partially accessible, with text-message features available but voice- and video-calling features blocked. In July users of FaceTime and other video-calling apps reported such services were blocked. In 2013 the CITC had announced it blocked the voice-calling app Viber and that it would "take appropriate action" against applications or services, including Skype and WhatsApp, if the proprietary services did not allow the government "lawful access" for monitoring purposes.

The CITC allows the public to submit requests to block or unblock specific sites. In 2010 the CITC stated it received more than 300,000 requests to block websites annually, citing an average of 200 requests daily to both block and unblock sites.

On July 3, the Ministry of Culture and Information blocked the website of the online news website *al-Marsad*. The ministry did not give a reason for the closure, and the block on the website was removed after five days.

The government reportedly collected information concerning the identity of persons peacefully expressing political, religious, or ideological opinions or beliefs online. On September 25, authorities arrested a man who used the nickname "Abu Sin" after internet video exchanges with a foreign female user circulated on social media. Authorities charged him with violating the anticyber crimes law, which in part prohibits the "production, preparation, transmission, or storage of material impinging on the public order, religious values, public morals, and privacy." He was released on bail after 10 days, according to media sources.

Academic Freedom and Cultural Events

The government censored public artistic expression, prohibited cinemas, and restricted public musical or theatrical performances other than those considered folkloric or special events approved by the government. Academics reportedly practiced self-censorship, and authorities prohibited professors and administrators at public universities from hosting meetings at their universities with foreign academics or diplomats without prior government permission. In October the Commission on Public Entertainment, established on May 7, hosted a public live dance performance in Riyadh and Jeddah and announced a series of entertainment performances as part of a new government-sponsored program under the auspices of the Vision 2030 economic reform agenda to foster live entertainment in the country.

b. Freedom of Peaceful Assembly and Association

The law does not provide for freedom of assembly and association, which the government severely limited.

Freedom of Assembly

The law requires a government permit for an organized public assembly of any type. The government categorically forbids participation in political protests or unauthorized public assemblies, and security forces reportedly arrested demonstrators and detained them for brief periods. Security forces, nonetheless, allowed a small number of unauthorized demonstrations throughout the country, despite a 2011 Ministry of Interior statement that demonstrations were banned and that it would take "all necessary measures" against those seeking to "disrupt order." The CSS reinforced the ministry's position, stating that "demonstrations are prohibited in this country" and explaining that "the correct way in sharia of realizing common interests is by advising."

There were an increased number of protests in the Qatif area of the Eastern Province in January and February following the execution of Shia cleric Nimr al-Nimr (see section 1.a.). Activists reported a significant presence of security forces. YouTube videos portrayed residents, largely Shia, protesting alleged systematic discrimination and neglect in government investment in physical and social infrastructure, including education, health care, and public facilities. Protests were largely nonviolent and decreased in size and number after February.

In contrast with previous years, there were no significant protests by family members of long-term detainees in Mabahith-run prisons.

The CPVPV and other security officers also restricted mixed gender gatherings of unrelated men and women in public and private spaces (see section 1.f.).

Freedom of Association

The law does not provide for freedom of association, and the government strictly limited this right. The government prohibited the establishment of political parties or any group it considered as opposing or challenging the regime. All associations must be licensed by the Ministry of Labor and Social Development and comply with its regulations. Some groups that advocated changing elements of the social or political order reported their licensing requests went unanswered for years, despite repeated inquiries. The ministry reportedly used arbitrary means, such as requiring unreasonable types and quantities of information, to delay and effectively deny licenses to associations. In November 2015 the cabinet passed a law authorizing the Ministry of Labor and Social Development to license NGOs. According to the International Center for Not-for-Profit Law, the Ministry of Labor and Social Development had registered 736 associations and 164 foundations as of April. The government previously provided licenses only to philanthropic and charitable societies; organizations that have social or research mandates required royal backing to avoid government interference or prosecution.

The few local NGOs that had operated without a license, including ACPRA, Union for Human Rights, and the Adala Center for Human Rights, ceased operating in 2013 and 2014 after authorities ordered them disbanded. By year's end the government had sentenced all 11 ACPRA founding members to prison terms. In 2014 ACPRA effectively ceased operations because of the continued harassment, investigation, prosecution, or detention of most of its members. While ACPRA maintained a presence on social media networks such as Twitter, the government severely curtailed its operations and closed down its website. In October, HRW reported that authorities filed charges against two activists, Mohammad al-Otaibi and Abdullah al-Attawi, for "forming an unlicensed organization" and other charges related to establishing a short-lived human rights organization called the Union for Human Rights, which was disbanded in 2013.

Government-chartered associations observed citizen-only limitations.

c. Freedom of Religion

See the Department of State's *International Religious Freedom Report* at www.state.gov/religiousfreedomreport/.

d. Freedom of Movement, Internally Displaced Persons, Protection of Refugees, and Stateless Persons

The law does not contain provisions for freedom of internal movement, foreign travel, emigration, and repatriation.

The government generally cooperated with the Office of the UN High Commissioner for Refugees (UNHCR) and other humanitarian organizations in providing protection and assistance to internally displaced persons, refugees, returning refugees, asylum seekers, stateless persons, and other persons of concern.

In-country Movement: The government generally did not restrict the free movement of male citizens within the country, but it severely restricted the movement of female citizens. While the guardianship system does not require a woman to have the permission of her male guardian (normally a father, husband, son, brother, grandfather, uncle, or other male relative) to move freely within the country, courts sometimes ruled that women should abide by a male guardian's request to stay at home by "occasionally upholding a guardian's right to obedience from his female dependents," according to an HRW report.

Authorities respected the right of citizens to change residence or workplace, provided they held a national identification card (NIC). The law requires all male citizens who are 15 or older to possess a NIC. In 2012 the Ministry of Interior announced it would start issuing NICs to all female citizens at the age of 15, phasing in the requirement over a seven-year period. In 2013 the ministry stated it had issued only 1.5 million NICs since 2002 to women. In December 2015 the ministry announced it began issuing NICs to widows and divorcees in possession of a death or divorce certificate. In August local media reported more than three million women over the age of 15 still did not possess a NIC. The 2015 population of women who were 15 or above was approximately 7.5 million, according to the General Authority for Statistics.

The government prohibited women from driving motor vehicles by refusing to issue licenses to them. In June authorities reportedly detained a woman for driving.

Foreign Travel: There are severe restrictions on foreign travel, including for women and members of minority groups. No one may leave the country without an exit visa and a passport. Women, minors (men younger than 21), and other dependents or foreign citizen workers under sponsorship require a male guardian's consent to travel abroad. According to Ministry of Interior regulations, a male guardian must apply for and collect a passport for women and minors. In October media reported that the Ministry of Justice reached an agreement with the General Directorate of Passports to remove the requirement for a deed of support document for widows and their children and to allow them to apply for passports with the directorate directly. A noncitizen wife needs permission from her husband to travel unless both partners sign a prenuptial agreement permitting the noncitizen wife to travel without the husband's permission; if a wife's guardian is deceased, a court may grant the permission. In June media reported that authorities granted 50 women permission to travel without a male guardian; five of the women were married to non-Saudi citizens. Government entities can ban the travel of citizens and noncitizens without trial, and male family members can "blacklist" women and minor children, prohibiting their travel.

Employers or sponsors controlled the departure of foreign workers and residents from the country; employers or sponsors were responsible for processing residence permits and exit visas on their behalf. Sponsors frequently held their employees' passports against the desires of the employees, despite a law specifically prohibiting this practice. Foreign workers typically provided sponsors with their residence permit before traveling in exchange for their passport to ensure the worker's return to their employer after their travel.

The government continued to impose international travel bans as part of criminal sentences. The government reportedly confiscated passports on occasion for political reasons and revoked the rights of some citizens to travel, often without providing them notification or opportunity to contest the restriction. Most travel bans reportedly involved individuals in court cases relating to financial and real estate disputes.

During the year the government banned several individuals engaged in human rights activism or political activities from foreign travel, in addition to hundreds of other travel bans promulgated by the courts. These included ACPRA members Eissa al-Hamid, Abdulaziz al-Shobaily, and Omar al-Sa'id as well as journalist Alaa Brinji.

Protection of Refugees

<u>Access to Asylum</u>: The law provides that the "state will grant political asylum if public interest so dictates." There are no regulations implementing this provision or UNHCR-managed refugee and asylum matters. The government permitted UNHCR-recognized refugees to stay in the country temporarily pending identification of a durable outcome, including third-country resettlement or voluntary repatriation. The government generally did not grant asylum or accept refugees for resettlement from third countries. Government policy is not to grant refugee status to persons in the country illegally, including those who have overstayed a pilgrimage visa. The government strongly encouraged persons

without residency to leave, and it threatened or imposed deportation. Access to naturalization was difficult for refugees.

The government did, however, grant six-month visas to Syrian and Yemeni nationals, and a royal decree allowed pro forma extensions of these visas. There was a nondeportation policy for Syrians and Yemenis. In May the Royal Court approved residency permits for Yemeni nationals who were in the country illegally prior to the beginning of coalition operations in Yemen. In the past year, the country normalized the status of 592,809 Yemenis, in addition to 1.5 million properly documented Yemenis, many of whom would be characterized as refugees but for the Saudi Arabian government's practice of avoiding using that term, bringing the total population of Yemenis living in Saudi Arabia to approximately two million. The government waived the costs and fees for visas, work permits, and permanent residency status applications for 2,570,972 Syrians who entered the country since 2011 because of the security situation in Syria. These included Syrians who entered the country without proper documentation who later normalized their status as well as individuals and families on visitor visas who were transiting to other countries.

Employment: Refugees and asylum seekers were generally unable to work legally. In February the Ministry of Labor and Social Development announced it would start allowing employers to apply online for an automatic work permit to be issued free of charge to Syrians and Yemenis who possessed a temporary visa and obtained a visitor card ("za'ir") from the Ministry of Interior. The renewable permits were valid for up to six months and tied to the validity period of their temporary visas; men between the ages of 18 and 60 were eligible to apply.

Access to Basic Services: The government reserves access to education, health care, public housing, courts and judicial procedures, legal services, and other social services to citizens only. A royal decree issued in 2012 permits all Syrians in Saudi Arabia free access to the educational system, and a separate decree issued in 2015 gives Yemenis in Saudi Arabia free access to schools. In 2015-16 the government enrolled and funded 141,406 Syrian students and 285,644 Yemeni students in local schools and provided college scholarships to 7,950 Syrians and 3,880 Yemenis. The UNHCR office in Riyadh provided a subsistence allowance covering basic services to a limited number of vulnerable families, based on a needs assessment. Authorities worked with UNHCR to provide medical treatment following a needs assessment. Since 2015 the government provided free health care to 47,000 Yemenis and paid for treatment of more than 3,426 injured Yemenis located in Saudi Arabia, Jordan, and Sudan.

Stateless Persons

The country had a significant number of habitual residents who were legally stateless, but data on the stateless population were incomplete and scarce.

Citizenship is legally derived only from the father. Children may be born stateless if they were born to an unmarried citizen mother who is not legally affiliated with the citizen father, even if the father recognized the child as his, or if the government did not authorize the marriage of a citizen father and a noncitizen mother prior to birth of the children. The nationality laws do not allow Saudi women married to foreign nationals to pass their nationality to their children, except in certain circumstances such as where fathers are unknown, stateless, of unknown nationality, or do not establish filiation. Sons of citizen mothers and noncitizen fathers may apply for citizenship once they turn 18 (if they were not already granted citizenship at birth under certain circumstances). Daughters can obtain citizenship only through marriage to a Saudi man. A child may lose legal identification and accompanying rights if authorities withdraw identification documents from a parent (possible when a naturalized parent denaturalizes voluntarily or loses citizenship through other acts). Since there is no codified personal-status law, judges make decisions regarding family matters based on their own interpretations of Islamic law.

In 2013 the government clarified regulations governing the status of non-Saudi men married to Saudi women. Foreign male spouses of female citizens are entitled to permanent residency in the country without needing a sponsor, and they receive free government education and medical benefits. These spouses are also counted in the quota of Saudis employed in private companies under the "nitaqaat," or labor quota system, which improves their employment prospects. Female citizens must also be between the ages of 30 and 55 in order to marry a non-Saudi man. Non-Saudi wives of Saudi men receive more rights if they have children resulting from their marriage with a Saudi man than if they do not. Male citizens must be between the ages of 40 and 65 in order to marry a non-Saudi woman. The extent to which those strictures were enforced was unclear, and there was anecdotal evidence that these were not uniformly enforced. Children of Saudi women who are married to foreign spouses receive permanent residency, but their residency status is revocable in the event of the death of the Saudi mother. In October the government issued a 17-point charter with additional regulations on marriage to non-Saudi citizens. Under the charter, a male citizen must earn 3,000 riyals ($800) per month and must own or rent an apartment or house before he can marry a noncitizen woman. The charter also states that, for female citizens, the age difference between them and any prospective non-Saudi spouse cannot exceed 10 years. On December 16, media reported that the government instituted a new policy requiring prospective foreign spouses to undergo a medical examination and drug testing prior to marriage to Saudi citizens.

UNHCR unofficially estimated there were 70,000 stateless persons in the country, almost all of whom were native-born residents known locally as "bidoon" (an Arabic word that means "without" [citizenship]). Bidoon are persons whose ancestors failed to obtain nationality, such as descendants of nomadic tribes not counted among the native tribes during the reign of the country's founder, King Abdulaziz; descendants of foreign-born fathers who arrived before there were laws regulating citizenship; and rural migrants whose parents failed to register their births. As noncitizens, bidoon are unable to obtain passports. The government sometimes denied them employment and educational opportunities, and their marginalized status made them among the poorest residents of the country. In recent years the Ministry of Education encouraged them to attend school. The government issues bidoon five-year residency permits to facilitate their social integration in government-provided health-care and other services, putting them on similar footing with sponsored foreign workers. In 2014 the General Directorate of Passports began to issue special identity cards to bidoon similar to residency permits issued to foreigners in the country, but with features entitling their holders to additional government services similar to those available to citizens.

There were also some Baloch, West Africans, and Rohingya Muslims from Burma, but only a portion of these communities was stateless. For example, many Rohingya had expired passports that their home government refused to renew. UNHCR estimated there were between 250,000 and 500,000 Rohingya in the country. During the year some of these individuals benefited from a program to correct their residency status; the government issued approximately 200,000 four-year residency permits by year's end. Only an estimated 2,000 individuals of Rohingya origin had Saudi citizenship. There also were between 300,000 and 400,000 Palestinian residents not registered as refugees.

Section 3. Freedom to Participate in the Political Process

The law does not provide citizens the ability to choose their government in free and fair periodic elections held by secret ballot and based on universal and equal suffrage; it establishes an absolute monarchy led by the Al Saud family as the political system. The law provides citizens the right to communicate with public authorities on any matter and establishes the government on the principle of consultation ("shura"). The king and senior officials, including ministers and regional governors, are required to be available by holding meetings ("majlis"), open-door events where in theory any male citizen or noncitizen may express an opinion or a grievance without the need for an appointment. Most government ministries and agencies had women's sections to interact with female citizens and noncitizens, and at least two regional governorates hired female employees to receive women's petitions and arrange meetings for women with complaints for, or requests of, the governor. Only select members of the ruling family have a voice in the choice of leaders, the composition of the government, or changes to the political system. The Allegiance Commission, composed of up to 35 senior princes appointed by the king, is formally responsible for selecting a king and crown prince upon the death or incapacitation of either.

Elections and Political Participation

Recent Elections: In December 2015 elections were held for two-thirds of the 3,159 seats on 284 municipal councils; the government appointed the remaining third. Women were allowed to vote and run as candidates for the first time. The voting age was also lowered universally to 18 years. The Ministry of Municipal and Rural Affairs actively encouraged women's participation in the municipal elections. According to the ministry, 131,188 women registered to vote (compared with 1,373,971 men registered in 2015 and previous election cycles), and 979 ran as candidates (compared with 5,938 men). Election regulations prohibited candidates from contesting under party affiliation. Twenty-one women won seats and 17 were appointed to seats, totaling approximately 1 percent of all available seats.

The NSHR observed the elections, and select international journalists were also permitted to observe. Independent polling station observers identified no irregularities with the election. Prior to the election, several candidates reported they were disqualified for "violating the rules and regulations," without further explanation. They had the right to appeal, and some were reinstated. Uniformed members of the security forces, including the military and police, were ineligible to vote.

Political Parties and Political Participation: There were no political parties or similar associations. The law does not protect the right of individuals to organize politically. The counterterrorism law's implementation regulations issued by the Ministry of Interior in 2014 explicitly banned a number of organizations that had political wings, including the Muslim Brotherhood, as regional and local terrorist groups. The government continued to regard human rights organizations, such as ACPRA, as illegal political movements and treated them accordingly.

<u>Participation of Women and Minorities</u>: Gender discrimination excluded women from many aspects of public life. Women slowly but increasingly participated in political life, albeit with significantly less status than men, in part due to guardianship laws requiring a male guardian's permission for legal decisions, restrictions on women candidates' contact with male voters in the 2016 elections, and the ban on women driving. In the December 2015 municipal elections, women made up less than 10 percent of the final list of registered voters, according to HRW. In March, Jeddah municipal council member Lama al-Sulaiman resigned after the ministry issued a decision requiring male and female council members to sit in separate rooms.

In 2013 the former king issued a royal decree changing the governance of the Consultative Council, the 150-person royally appointed body that advises the king and may propose but not pass laws. The changes mandate that women constitute no less than 20 percent of the membership of the Consultative Council. In accordance with the law, in 2013 the council inducted 30 women as full members. On December 2, the king issued a new decree reconstituting the 150-member Consultative Council and keeping the number of women members at 30.

Women were routinely excluded from formal decision-making positions in both government and the private sector, although some women attained leadership positions in business and served in senior advisory positions within government ministries. Women's ability to practice law was severely limited; there were no women on the High Court or Supreme Judicial Council and no women judges or public prosecutors. In August the Ministry of Justice announced that women could not be appointed as public notaries in the courts. The government, however, continued to issue licenses to female lawyers. In September Ministry of Justice officials announced that, while there were no women employed in their agency, the government had granted 39 law licenses to women during the year, approximately 8 percent of the total number of 512 licenses, bringing the total number of women licensed to practice law in the country to 102. The ministry allowed an additional 450 female law graduates to work in internships.

During the year the most senior position held by a woman in government was vice president for women's affairs of the General Sports Authority.

The country had an increasing number of female diplomats. Bureaucratic procedures largely restricted women working in the security services to employment in women's prisons, at women's universities, and in clerical positions in police stations, where they were responsible for visually identifying other women for law enforcement purposes. According to the National Transformation Program, 39.8 percent of government employees (excluding the military) were women, and women occupied 1.27 percent of top government positions.

No laws prevent males from minority groups from participating in political life on the same basis as other male citizens. Societal discrimination, however, marginalized the Shia population, and tribal factors and longstanding traditions continued to dictate many individual appointments to positions. Unofficially, government authorities will not appoint a Bedouin tribesman to a high-ranking cabinet-level position, and Bedouins can only reach the rank of major general in the armed forces. All cabinet members who were tribal were members of urbanized "Hamael" tribes rather than Bedouin tribes. While the religious affiliation of Consultative Council members was not known publicly, the council included an estimated seven or eight Shia members. In contrast with previous years, the cabinet contained one religious minority member. In 2014 the late King Abdullah appointed Mohammad bin Faisal Abu Saq, a Shia, as minister of state and member of the cabinet for consultative council affairs. Multiple municipal councils in the Eastern Province, where most Shia were concentrated, had large proportions of Shia as members to reflect the local population, including a majority in Qatif and 50 percent in al-Hasa. Eastern Province Shia judges dealing with intra-Shia personal status and family laws operated specialized courts.

Section 4. Corruption and Lack of Transparency in Government

The law provides criminal penalties for official corruption. The government did not implement the law effectively; some officials engaged in corrupt practices with impunity, and perceptions of corruption persisted in some sectors.

Government employees who accept bribes face 10 years in prison or fines up to one million riyals ($267,000). The National Anticorruption Commission ("Nazaha"), established by King Abdullah in 2011, was responsible for promoting transparency and combating all forms of financial and administrative corruption. The commission's ministerial-level director reported directly to the king. In February 2015 the Shura Council censured Nazaha for its failure to prosecute a sufficient number of corruption cases. The council also stated that the public did not believe Nazaha could handle its responsibility to investigate and punish corruption. The Control and Investigation Board remains responsible for investigating financial malfeasance, and the BIPP has the lead on all criminal investigations. The HRC also responded to and researched complaints of corruption. Provincial governors and other members of the royal family paid compensation to victims of corruption during weekly majlis meetings where citizens raised complaints.

Corruption: Nazaha continued operations and referred cases of possible public corruption to the BIPP. In November, Nazaha announced that it had found irregularities in the appointment of a cabinet minister's son to the Ministry of Municipal and Rural Affairs. In July, Nazaha declared it was investigating an official of the Ministry of Transportation for granting 14 million riyals ($3,730,000) in compensation to his relatives.

Financial Disclosure: Public officials were not subject to financial disclosure laws.

Public Access to Information: The law does not provide for, and there is no right to, public access to government information, such as ministerial budgets or allocations to members of the royal family.

Section 5. Governmental Attitude Regarding International and Nongovernmental Investigation of Alleged Violations of Human Rights

The law provides that "the State shall protect human rights in accordance with Islamic sharia." The government restricted the activities of domestic and international human rights organizations. The government did not allow international human rights NGOs to be based in the country but allowed representatives to visit on a limited basis. International human rights and humanitarian NGOs reported that the government was at times unresponsive to requests for information and did not establish a clear mechanism for communication with NGOs on both domestic human rights issues and on issues relating to the conflict in Yemen. There were no transparent standards governing visits by international NGO representatives. The HRC stated that the government welcomed visits by legitimate, unbiased human rights groups but added the government could not act on the "hundreds of requests" it received, in part because it was cumbersome to decide which domestic agencies would be their interlocutor.

The government often cooperated with and sometimes accepted the recommendations of the NSHR, the sole government-licensed domestic human rights organization. The NSHR accepted requests for assistance and complaints about government actions affecting human rights.

The government viewed unlicensed local human rights groups with suspicion, frequently blocking their websites and charging their founders with founding and operating an unlicensed organization. ACPRA applied for a license in 2008, which authorities did not grant. The government initially allowed its unlicensed operation, but it remained unclear which activities the group could undertake without risking punishment. For example, the group was unable to raise operating funds legally, which limited its activities. In 2013 a court ordered the dissolution of ACPRA and confiscation of its assets (see section 2.b., Freedom of Association).

Government Human Rights Bodies: The HRC is part of the government and requires the permission of the Ministry of Foreign Affairs before meeting with diplomats, academics, or researchers with international human rights organizations. The HRC president has ministerial status and reports to the king. The well-resourced HRC was effective in highlighting problems and registering and responding to the complaints it received, but its capacity to effect change was more limited. The HRC worked directly with the Royal Diwan and the cabinet, with a committee composed of representatives of the Consultative Council and the Ministries of Labor and Social Development and Interior, and with Consultative Council committees for the judiciary, Islamic affairs, and human rights.

During the year the HRC and NSHR were more outspoken in areas deemed less politically sensitive, including child abuse, child marriage, prison conditions, and cases of individuals detained beyond their prescribed prison sentences. They avoided topics, such as protests or cases of political activists or reformists, that would require directly confronting government authorities. The HRC board's 18 full-time members included four women and at least three Shia; they received and responded to complaints submitted by their constituencies, including problems related to persons with disabilities, religious freedom, and women's rights. The Consultative Council's Human Rights Committee also actively followed cases and included women and Shia among its members; a woman served as chairperson of the committee.

Section 6. Discrimination, Societal Abuses, and Trafficking in Persons

Women

<u>Rape and Domestic Violence</u>: Rape is a criminal offense under sharia with a wide range of penalties from flogging to execution. The law does not recognize spousal rape as a crime. The government enforced the law based on its interpretation of sharia, and courts often punished victims as well as perpetrators for illegal "mixing of genders," even when there was no conviction for rape. Victims also had to prove that the rape was committed, and women's testimony in court is, in certain cases, worth half the weight of that of a man. Due to these legal and social penalties, authorities brought few cases to trial. The government did not maintain public records on prosecutions, convictions, or punishments.

Statistics on incidents of rape were not available, but press reports and observers indicated rape was a serious problem. Moreover, most rape cases were likely unreported because victims faced societal and familial reprisal, including diminished marriage opportunities, criminal sanction up to imprisonment, or accusations of adultery or sexual relations outside of marriage, which are punishable under sharia.

The 2013 law against domestic violence provides a framework for the government to prevent and protect victims of violence in the home. The law defines domestic abuse broadly and criminalizes domestic abuse with penalties of one month to one year of imprisonment or a fine of 5,000 to 50,000 riyals ($1,330 to $13,300) unless a court provides a harsher sentence.

Researchers stated that domestic violence might be seriously underreported, making it difficult to gauge the magnitude of the problem, which they believed to be widespread. The Ministry of Justice received 1,498 cases of domestic violence over the previous Hijri calendar year, according to media reports. In December 2015 the Ministry of Labor and Social Development handled 8,016 cases of physical and psychological abuse, 57.5 percent of which involved spousal abuse, according to media reports. The NSHR's 2015 annual report noted that the organization investigated 295 cases of domestic violence and violations of women's rights. The National Family Safety Program, a private charity organization founded in 2005 to spread awareness and combat domestic violence, including child abuse, continued to report abuse cases.

Officials stated that the government did not clearly define domestic violence and procedures concerning cases, including thresholds for investigation or prosecution, and thus enforcement varied from one government body to another. Some women's rights advocates were critical of investigations of domestic violence, claiming investigators were hesitant to enter a home without permission from the head of household, who may also be the male perpetrator. Some activists also claimed that authorities often did not investigate or prosecute cases involving domestic violence, instead encouraging victims and perpetrators to reconcile in order to keep families intact regardless of reported abuse. Violence included a broad spectrum of abuse. There were reports of police or judges returning women directly to their abusers, most of whom were the women's legal guardians.

The government made efforts to combat domestic violence, and during the year the King Abdulaziz Center for National Dialogue held workshops and distributed educational materials on peaceful conflict resolution between spouses and in families. The government supported family-protection shelters. The HRC received complaints of domestic abuse and referred them to other government offices. The HRC advised complainants and offered legal assistance to some female litigants. The organization provided services for children of female complainants and litigants and distributed publications supporting women's rights in education, health care, development, and the workplace. On March 29, the Ministry of Labor and Social Development announced the launch of a domestic violence call center, noting that the center had received 1,890 calls in its first three days of operations.

Female Genital Mutilation/Cutting (FGM/C): FGM/C was not a common practice in the country, particularly among the Saudi population, as the official government interpretation of sharia prohibits the practice.

Other Harmful Traditional Practices: There were no known deaths involving dowry, honor killings, or other harmful practices targeting women during the year.

Sexual Harassment: The extent of sexual harassment was difficult to measure, with little media reporting and no government data. The government's interpretation of sharia guides courts on cases of sexual harassment. Nonetheless, female workers reported sexual harassment and discrimination. Employers in many sectors maintained separate male and female workspaces where feasible, in accordance with law.

Reproductive Rights: Couples and individuals have the right to decide the number, spacing, and timing of their children; manage their reproductive health; and have access to the information and means to do so, free from discrimination, coercion, and violence. Although no legal barriers prevent access to contraception, constraints on mobility and economic resources as well as social pressure for large families limited many women. According to 2016 estimates by the UN Population

Fund, 31 percent of women between the ages of 15 and 49 used a modern method of contraceptives and 24 percent of women had an unmet need for family planning.

<u>Discrimination</u>: Women continued to face significant discrimination under law and custom, and many remained uninformed about their rights. To increase awareness, on July 4, a female lawyer launched an Arabic mobile phone application, "Know Your Rights." The application contained resources for legal aid as well as answers to frequently asked questions on issues such as divorce, child custody, guardianship, disability, and domestic violence.

The law does not provide for the same legal status and rights for women as for men, and since there is no codified personal-status law, judges made decisions regarding family matters based on their interpretations of Islamic law. Although they may legally own property and are entitled to financial support from their guardian, women have fewer political or social rights than men, and society treated them as unequal members in the political and social spheres. The guardianship system requires that every woman have a close male relative as her "guardian" with the legal authority to approve her travel outside of the country. A guardian also has authority to approve some types of business licenses and study at a university or college. Women can make their own determinations concerning hospital care. Women can work without their guardian's permission, but most employers required women to have such permission. A husband who verbally (rather than through a court process) divorces his wife or refuses to sign final divorce papers continues to be her legal guardian.

The overall percentage of female workforce participation was 21 percent, according to the World Economic Forum's *Gender Gap Report 2015*. The law does not require equal pay for equal work.

Nationality law discriminates against women, who cannot directly transmit citizenship to their children, particularly if the children's father is a noncitizen (see section 2.d. and section 6, Children). The country's interpretation of sharia prohibits women from marrying non-Muslims, but men may marry Christians and Jews. Women require government permission to marry noncitizens; men must be older than 25 to marry a foreigner and must obtain government permission if they intend to marry citizens from countries other than Gulf Cooperation Council member states (Saudi Arabia, Bahrain, Kuwait, Oman, Qatar, and the United Arab Emirates). Regulations prohibit men from marrying women from Pakistan, Bangladesh, Chad, and Burma. The government additionally required Saudi men wishing to marry a second wife who is a foreigner to submit documentation attesting to the fact that his first wife is disabled, has a chronic disease, or is sterile.

Widespread societal exclusion enforced by, but not limited to, state institutions restricted women from using many public facilities. The law requires women usually to sit in separate, specially designated family sections. They frequently cannot consume food in restaurants that do not have such sections. Women risk arrest for riding in a private vehicle driven by a male who is not an employee (such as a hired chauffeur or taxi driver) or a close male relative. Cultural norms enforced by state institutions require women to wear an "abaya" (a loose-fitting, full-length black cloak) in public. The CPVPV also generally expected Muslim women to cover their hair and non-Muslim women from Asian and African countries to comply more fully with local customs of dress than non-Muslim Western women.

On December 12, media reported that Malak al-Shehri was detained after posting a photograph of herself on Twitter on November 28, dressed in a jacket (rather an abaya) with her hair uncovered (without a "hijab") on a busy street in Riyadh. Riyadh police claimed that the CPVPV had reported al-Shehri's actions to them and that her detention was in line with the duty of the police to monitor against violations of general morals and illegal actions. Al-Shehri was released on December 19.

Women also faced discrimination in courts, where in most cases the testimony of one man equals that of two women. All judges are male, and women faced restrictions on their practice of law. In divorce proceedings, women must demonstrate legally specified grounds for divorce, but men can divorce without giving cause. In doing so, men must pay immediately an amount of money agreed at the time of the marriage that serves as a one-time alimony payment. Men can be forced, however, to make subsequent alimony payments by court order. The government began implementing an identification system based on fingerprints that was designed to provide women more reliable access to courts. The previous system required women to present themselves at court in the presence of a male relative to prove their identity if they declined to unveil their faces.

Women faced discrimination under family law. For example, a woman needs a guardian's permission to marry or must seek a court order in the case of "adhl" (male guardians refusing to approve the marriage of women under their charge). In such adhl cases, the judge assumes the role of the guardian and can approve the marriage. In February the Ministry of Justice reported that courts received 128 adhl cases during the previous three months.

Courts award custody of children when they attain a specified age (seven years for boys and nine years for girls) to the divorced husband or the deceased husband's family. In numerous cases former husbands prevented divorced noncitizen women from visiting their children. Inheritance laws also discriminate against women, since daughters receive half the inheritance awarded to their brothers.

According to recent surveys, women constituted more than half of university students, although segregated education through university level was the norm. The only exceptions to segregation in higher education were medical schools at the undergraduate level and the King Abdullah University of Science and Technology, a graduate-level research university, where women worked jointly with men, were not required to wear a veil, and drove cars on campus. Other universities, such as al-Faisal University in Riyadh, offered partially segregated classes with students receiving instruction from the same teacher and able to participate together in class discussion, but with the women and men physically separated by dividers.

Children

Birth Registration: Citizenship derives from the father, and only the father can register a birth. There were cases of authorities denying children of citizen parents public services, including education and health care, because the government failed to register the birth entirely or had not registered it immediately, sometimes because the father failed to report the birth (see section 2.d., Stateless Persons). Children of Saudi women who are married to foreign spouses receive permanent residency, but their residency status is revocable in the event of the death of the Saudi mother.

Child Abuse: Abuse of children occurred. In 2015 the NSHR registered 154 cases of violence against children, according to its annual report. In March local media reported a National Family Safety Program study that found 60 percent of domestic abuse complaints received involved children who suffered some form of physical abuse, with 5 to 10 percent of children exposed to physical violence and 80 percent of teenagers exposed to various forms of physical and psychological abuse.

In June the Riyadh Criminal Court sentenced a man to eight years in prison and 700 lashes for beating his seven-year-old daughter to death.

<u>Early and Forced Marriage</u>: There was one report during the year of child marriage; in prior years the practice was almost entirely limited to rural areas. The law does not specify a minimum age for marriage, although Ministry of Justice guidelines referred marriage applications to sharia courts to determine the validity of a marriage when the bride was under the age of 16. In March a court ordered the annulment of a marriage between a girl who was under the age of 15 and an 84-year-old man. According to some senior religious leaders, girls as young as 10 may marry. Families sometimes arranged such marriages to settle family debts without the consent of the child. The HRC and NSHR monitored cases of child marriages, which they reported were rare or at least rarely reported, and took steps to prevent them from being consummated. Media reports quoted judges as saying the majority of child marriage cases in the country involved Syrian girls, followed by smaller numbers of Egyptians and Yemenis. There were media reports that some men traveled abroad to find brides, some of whom were legally minors. The application for a marriage license must record the bride's age, and registration of the marriage is a legal prerequisite for consummation. The government reportedly instructed marriage registrars not to register marriages involving children.

<u>Female Genital Mutilation/Cutting (FGM/C)</u>: FGM/C was not a common practice for children in the country (see Women above).

<u>Sexual Exploitation of Children</u>: The anticyber crimes law stipulates that punishment for such crimes, including the preparation, publication, and promotion of material for pornographic sites, may be no less than two and one-half years' imprisonment or a fine of 1.5 million riyals ($400,000) if the crime includes the exploitation of minors. The law does not define a minimum age for consensual sex.

<u>International Child Abductions</u>: The country is not a party to the 1980 Hague Convention on the Civil Aspects of International Child Abduction. See the Department of State's *Annual Report on International Parental Child Abduction* at travel.state.gov/content/childabduction/en/legal/compliance.html.

Anti-Semitism

There were no known Jewish citizens and no statistics available concerning the religious denominations of foreigners.

Cases of government-employed imams using anti-Jewish language in their sermons were rare and occurred without authorization by government authorities. The law requires government-employed imams to give all sermons delivered in mosques in the country. They must deliver sermons vetted and cleared by the Ministry of Islamic Affairs. During the year the ministry issued periodic circulars to clerics and imams in mosques directing them to include messages on the principles of justice, equality, and tolerance and to encourage rejection of bigotry and all forms of racial discrimination in their sermons. According to the ministry, no imams publicly espoused intolerant views warranting dismissal during the year. Unauthorized imams continued to employ intolerant views in their sermons.

There were reports of anti-Semitic materials available at government-sponsored book fairs.

The government's multi-year Tatweer project to revise textbooks, curricula, and teaching methods to promote tolerance and remove content disparaging religions other than Islam began in 2007. As of 2013, the program had received more than 11 billion riyals ($2.9 billion) to revise the curriculum, and the government had developed new curricula and textbooks for at least grades four through 10. Despite these efforts, some intolerant material remained in textbooks used in schools.

Editorial cartoons exhibited anti-Semitism characterized by stereotypical images of Jews along with Jewish symbols, particularly at times of heightened political tension with Israel. Anti-Semitic comments by journalists, academics, and clerics appeared in the media.

Trafficking in Persons

See the Department of State's *Trafficking in Persons Report* at www.state.gov/j/tip/rls/tiprpt/.

Persons with Disabilities

The law does not prohibit discrimination against persons with physical, sensory, intellectual, and mental disabilities in employment, education, air travel and other transportation, access to health care, the judicial system, or the provision of other state services or other areas. The law does not require public accessibility to buildings, information, and communications. Newer commercial buildings often included such access, as did some newer government buildings. Children with disabilities could attend government-supported schools.

Information about patterns of abuse of persons with disabilities in prisons and educational and mental health institutions was not widely available. Persons with disabilities could generally participate in civic affairs, and there were no legal restrictions that prevented persons with disabilities from voting in municipal council elections, although lack of accessibility of buildings, information, and communications likely limited some persons with disabilities from participating fully. In 2013 the HRC appointed four experts to work as advocates for persons with disabilities in the kingdom and to respond to complaints of discrimination; their work expanded during the year to include participation in international conferences on discrimination against persons with disabilities. The King Salman Center for Disability Research, a nonprofit research foundation, continued to conduct laboratory and field research on a range of disability and quality of life issues. The Ministry of Labor and Social Development was responsible for protecting the rights of persons with disabilities. Vocational rehabilitation projects and social care programs increasingly brought persons with disabilities into the mainstream. Persons with disabilities were elected and appointed as members of municipal councils in December 2015, and two individuals with disabilities also served on the consultative Shura Council, which was reconstituted on December 2.

National/Racial/Ethnic Minorities

Although racial discrimination is illegal, societal discrimination against members of national, racial, and ethnic minorities was a problem. There was also discrimination based on tribal or nontribal lineage. Descendants of former slaves in the country, who have African lineage, faced discrimination in both employment and society. There was formal and informal discrimination, especially racial discrimination, against foreign workers from Africa and Asia. The tolerance campaign of the King Abdulaziz Center for National Dialogue sought to address some of these problems, and it provided training during the year to combat discrimination against national, racial, or ethnic groups.

The Shia minority continued to suffer social, legal, economic, and political discrimination. To address the problem, in recent years the Ministries of Defense and Interior and the National Guard included antidiscrimination training in courses run by the King Abdulaziz Center for National Dialogue for police and other law enforcement officers (for additional information, see Other Societal Violence and Discrimination).

Acts of Violence, Discrimination, and Other Abuses Based on Sexual Orientation and Gender Identity

Under sharia as interpreted in the country, consensual same-sex sexual conduct is punishable by death or flogging, depending on the perceived seriousness of the case. It is illegal for men "to behave like women" or to wear women's clothes and vice versa. Due to social conventions and potential persecution, lesbian, gay, bisexual, transgender, and intersex (LGBTI) organizations did not operate openly, nor were there gay rights advocacy events of any kind. There were reports of official societal discrimination, physical violence, and harassment based on sexual orientation or gender identity in employment, housing, access to education, and health care. Stigma or intimidation acted to limit reports of incidents of abuse. Sexual orientation and gender identity could constitute the basis for harassment, blackmail, or other actions.

There were no government efforts to address potential discrimination. In March newspapers quoted BIPP officials as stating the bureau would seek death sentences for anyone using social media to solicit homosexual acts. There were no reports, however, that BIPP sought death sentences in LGBTI cases during the year.

Local media reported in April that the Jeddah Criminal Court had processed 60 cases of LGBTI individuals over the past year. In April a newspaper reported that the Jeddah Criminal Court sentenced a citizen to six months in prison and 180 lashes after he was convicted of "promoting homosexuality on social media networks." In January a newspaper reported that the CPVPV arrested two men in Riyadh who were reportedly married and living together.

HIV and AIDS Social Stigma

There were no reports of societal violence or discrimination against persons with HIV/AIDS. By law the government deported foreign workers who tested positive for HIV/AIDS upon arrival or who tested positive when hospitalized for other reasons. There was no indication that HIV-positive foreigners failed to receive antiretroviral treatment or that authorities isolated them during the year. The Ministry of Health's HIV/AIDS program worked to fight stigma and discrimination against persons with HIV/AIDS.

Other Societal Violence or Discrimination

Societal violence and discrimination against the country's Shia minority continued. Multiple attacks on Shia mosques or community halls occurred (see section 1.a.). As a result of the attacks, there was increased cooperation between government security forces and local Shia volunteer security committees. Government officials and the public widely condemned all attacks.

Section 7. Worker Rights

a. Freedom of Association and the Right to Collective Bargaining

The law does not provide for the right of workers to form and join independent unions. The law does not provide for the right to collective bargaining or the right to conduct legal strikes. The law does not prohibit antiunion discrimination or require reinstatement of workers fired for union activity.

The government did not respect freedom of association and the right to collective bargaining. There were no labor unions in the country, and workers faced potential dismissal, imprisonment, or, in the case of migrant workers, deportation for union activities. The High Commission for the Settlement of Labor Disputes, a specialized committee under the Ministry of Labor and Social Development, is a labor court that hears employment-related disputes in the private sector.

The government allowed citizen-only labor committees in workplaces with more than 100 employees but it placed undue limitations on freedom of association and was heavily involved in the formation and activities of these committees. For example, the Ministry of Labor and Social Development approves the committee members and authorizes ministry and employer representatives to attend committee meetings. Committee members must submit the minutes of meetings to management and then transmit them to the minister; the ministry can dissolve committees if they violate regulations or are deemed to threaten public security. Regulations limit committees to making recommendations to company management regarding only improvements to working conditions, health and safety, productivity, and training programs. In its 2015 annual report, the NSHR registered 214 labor-related complaints.

b. Prohibition of Forced or Compulsory Labor

The law prohibits forced or compulsory labor, but the government did not effectively enforce legal protections for migrant workers. Forced labor occurred, especially among migrant workers--notably domestic servants--and children.

Conditions indicative of forced labor experienced by foreign workers included withholding of passports, nonpayment of wages, restrictions on movement, and verbal, physical, and sexual abuse. Amendments to the labor law, including prohibitions on the confiscation of passports and nonpayment of wages, went into effect in October 2015. Violations of labor laws resulted in fines of up to one million riyals ($267,000), prison terms up to 15 years, and restrictions on the entity's ability to recruit foreign workers. Many noncitizen workers, particularly domestic employees who were not covered under the labor law, were not able to exercise their right to end their contractual work. An employer may require a trainee to work for him or her upon completion of training for a period not to exceed twice the duration of the training or one year, whichever is longer.

Restrictive sponsorship laws increased workers' vulnerability to forced labor conditions and made many foreign workers reluctant to report abuse. The contract system does not allow workers to change employers or leave the country without the written consent of the employer. During the year numerous migrant workers reported being laid off, sometimes after months of nonpayment of salaries. Some remained stranded in the country because they were unable to pay required exit visa fees. A few countries that contributed migrant labor to the country in the past prohibited their citizens from seeking work there after widespread reports of worker abuse.

The government continued implementation of the Wage Protection System (WPS), which required employers to pay foreign workers through bank transfers, thereby allowing the Ministry of Labor and Social Development to ensure workers were paid appropriately. Through October the ministry shut down 1,441 companies for failing to comply with the WPS. The ministry reported 9,500 cases in which foreign migrants were working for employers without legal sponsorship.

Throughout the year the government strictly implemented measures to limit the number of noncitizen workers in the kingdom. The government also penalized Hajj tourist agencies that engaged in human trafficking and local companies that abused the country's visa laws to bring individuals into the country for reasons other than to employ them directly. During the period between April 2015, and March 31, government enforcement improved, with a reported 257 percent increase in the number of traffickers convicted and a 1,054 percent increase in the number of victims identified. Many individuals either left their legal sponsors' employment or stayed on after expiration of their work visas and residence permits. A smaller number came as religious pilgrims and overstayed their visas.

Because of their undocumented status, many persons in the country were susceptible to forced labor, substandard wages, and deportation by authorities.

Also see the Department of State's *Trafficking in Persons Report* at www.state.gov/j/tip/rls/tiprpt/.

c. Prohibition of Child Labor and Minimum Age for Employment

The law provides that no person younger than 15 may legally work unless that person is the sole source of support for the family. Children between the ages of 13 and 15 may work if the job is not harmful to health or growth and does not interfere with schooling. The law provides that hazardous operations or harmful industries may not employ legal minors; children under the age of 18 may not be employed for shifts exceeding six hours a day. There is no minimum age for workers employed in family-owned businesses or other areas considered extensions of the household, such as farming, herding, and domestic service.

The HRC and NSHR are responsible for monitoring enforcement of child labor laws. There was little information on government efforts to enforce relevant laws or actions to prevent or eliminate child labor during the year. Authorities most commonly enforced the law in response to complaints of children begging on the streets.

Most child labor involved children from other countries, including Yemen and Ethiopia, forced into begging rings, street vending, and work in family businesses.

d. Discrimination with Respect to Employment and Occupation

Labor laws and regulations do not prohibit discrimination on the basis of race, color, sex, religion, political opinion, national origin or citizenship, social origin, disability, sexual orientation or gender identity, age, language, or HIV-positive status. Discrimination with respect to employment and occupation occurred with respect to all these categories.

The Ministry of Labor and Social Development explicitly approved and encouraged the employment of women in specific sectors, particularly in government, but women faced many discriminatory regulations. The third-quarter 2016 *Labor Force Survey* report by the General Authority for Statistics found that Saudi women (15 years of age and above) constituted 6 percent of the country's total employed and unemployed workforce (Saudi and non-Saudi, 15 years of age and above). The same report estimated that women, both Saudi and foreign, represented 12 percent of all employed persons (15 years of age and above) in the country. Rules limited the type of work women were allowed to perform, required them to wear a veil in most workplaces, and enforced gender segregation in the workplace on penalty of fines. The labor dispute settlement bodies did not register any cases of discrimination.

Amendments to the labor law that went into effect in October 2015 included relaxing some discriminatory provisions, such as requiring strict gender-segregation. They also allowed women to work in hazardous or dangerous jobs. There is no regulation requiring equal pay for equal work. In the private sector, the average monthly wage of Saudi women workers was 58 percent of the average monthly wage of Saudi men (see section 6, Women).

Regulations ban women from 24 professions, mostly in heavy industry, but create guidelines for women to telework. Nevertheless, some factories and manufacturing facilities, particularly in the Eastern Province, employed men and women, who worked separate shifts during different hours of the day. Despite gender segregation, the law grants women the right to obtain business licenses with the approval of their guardians, and women frequently obtained licenses in fields that might require them to supervise foreign workers, interact with male clients, or deal with government officials. In medical settings and the energy industry, women and men worked together, and in some instances women supervised male employees. Women who work in establishments with 50 or more female employees have the right to maternity leave and childcare.

Discrimination with respect to religious beliefs occurred in the workplace. Members of the Shia community complained of discrimination based on their religion and had difficulty securing or being promoted in government positions. Shia were significantly underrepresented in national security-related positions, including the Ministries of Defense and Interior and the National Guard. In predominantly Shia areas, Shia representation was higher in the ranks of traffic police, municipalities, and public schools. A very small number of Shia occupied high-level positions in government-owned companies and government agencies (see section 3, Participation of Women and Minorities). Shia were also underrepresented in employment in primary, secondary, and higher education.

Discrimination against Asian and African migrant workers occurred (see section 6, National/Racial/Ethnic Minorities). The King Abdulaziz Center for National Dialogue continued programs that sought to address some of these problems and provided training during the year to combat discrimination against national, racial, or ethnic groups. There were numerous cases of assault on foreign workers and reports of worker abuse. Government policies designed to increase the number of citizens in the workforce intentionally raised the costs of hiring migrant workers, which made it more difficult for them to find work.

Informal discrimination in employment and occupation occurred on the basis of sex, gender, race, religion, and sexual orientation or gender identity.

e. Acceptable Conditions of Work

The monthly minimum wage for public-sector employees was 3,000 riyals ($800). There was no private-sector minimum wage for foreign workers; the government's "Nitaqaat" (Saudization) program effectively set a general minimum private-sector wage for citizens at 3,000 riyals ($800) per month.

The Commission for the Settlement of Labor Disputes actively prosecuted cases against employers of citizens, with most outcomes favoring the employee. Prosecution of employers of noncitizens occurred with less frequency, and most verdicts reportedly favored the employer. The Ministry of Labor and Social Development also has the ability to arbitrate reconciliation between an employer and employee in a dispute. Labor regulations ostensibly apply to all workers in the public and private sectors, other than domestic servants (covered by a separate law). The regulations provide for a 48-hour standard workweek at regular pay, a weekly 24-hour rest period (normally on Fridays, although the employer may grant it on another day), and time-and-a-half pay for overtime, with a maximum of 12 additional hours per week for private-sector employees. The regulations do not distinguish between different types of employment. To protect laborers working out of doors, the government also imposed a midday work ban during the hottest parts of the day during the summer. The Ministry of Labor and Social Development registered 966 violations across 829 establishments during the year where companies violated the government's midday work ban during the summer months. The public-sector workweek is 35 hours with two rest days per week.

In 2013 the cabinet approved regulations to govern the work relationship between employers and domestic workers, including the creation of a dispute mechanism to settle financial claims. Under these regulations, the employer and the employee must have a written agreement outlining the worker's duties and rights that would then be the basis for legal action should either party fail to uphold the contract. If an employer commits a violation, the punishment could include a one-year recruitment ban, a 2,000 riyal ($530) fine, or both, with increasing penalties for repeat offenses. Domestic workers violating their contract could be assessed a similar fine and prohibited from working in the country.

The 2015 labor law protects workers' rights in the private sector and seeks to improve the work environment with new safety and welfare standards. The new provisions also provide assistance for workers seeking new employment after their contract terminates and provides for women to receive maternity leave.

An estimated 7.41 million noncitizens, including approximately 666,000 noncitizen women, made up approximately 57 percent of the labor force, according to the General Authority for Statistics third-quarter 2016 *Labor Force Survey*. Legal workers generally negotiated and agreed to work conditions prior to their arrival in the country, in accordance with the contract requirements contained in the labor law.

The law provides penalties of between 500 and 1,000 riyals ($133 and $267) for bringing foreigners into the country to work in any service, including domestic service, without following the required procedures and obtaining a permit. Local press reports indicated the ministry conducted 124,892 site visits and inspectors found more than 34,000 violations of labor law in the period between November 2014 and September 2015. The most commonly cited violation was failure to adhere to the seasonal prohibition against working in direct sun.

The labor law provides for regular safety inspections and enables Ministry of Labor-appointed inspectors to examine materials used or handled in industrial and other operations and to submit samples of suspected hazardous materials or substances to government laboratories. The Ministry of Health's Occupational Health Service Directorate worked with the Ministry of Labor on health and safety matters. Regulations require employers to protect some workers from job-related hazards and disease, although some violations occurred. These regulations did not cover farmers, herdsmen, domestic servants, or workers in family-operated businesses. Foreign nationals privately reported frequent failures to enforce health and safety standards. The Ministry of Labor employed nearly 1,000 labor inspectors.

The law requires that a citizen or business sponsor most foreign workers in order for them to obtain legal work and residency status, although the requirement exempts Syrian and Yemeni nationals who overstayed their visas. The Ministry of Labor and Social Development implemented measures allowing noncitizen workers to switch their employer to a new employer or company that employed a sufficient quota of Saudi nationals. Despite these revised measure, some workers were unaware of the new regulations and had to remain with their sponsor until completion of their contract or seek the assistance of their embassy to return home. There were also instances in which sponsors bringing noncitizen workers into the country failed to provide them with a residency permit, which undermined the workers' ability to access government services or navigate the court system in the event of grievances. Sponsors with commercial or labor disputes with foreign employees also could ask authorities to prohibit the employees from departing the country until the dispute was resolved. In 2014, however, the government announced that workers who fled their employers would not be jailed or forced to return to their employers to obtain an exit visa, provided they cooperated with their respective embassies within a 72-hour period and had no criminal charges or outstanding fines against them.

The Migrant Workers' Welfare Department of the Ministry of Labor and Social Development is responsible for addressing cases of abuse and exploitation of migrant workers. Noncitizen workers were able to submit complaints and seek help in 37 offices throughout the country. The Ministry of Labor and Social Development reportedly maintained a database of abusive employers and banned individuals and companies who mistreated noncitizen workers from sponsoring such workers for up to five years. There was no data on enforcement of these policies.

Bilateral labor agreements set conditions on foreign workers' minimum wage, housing, benefits including leave and medical care, and other topics. These provisions were not necessarily drafted in line with international standards, and they varied depending on the sending country's relative bargaining leverage. The labor law and the law against trafficking provide penalties for abuse of such workers.

The government engaged in news campaigns highlighting the plight of abused workers, trained law enforcement and other officials to combat trafficking in persons, and worked with the embassies of labor-sending countries to disseminate information about labor rights to foreign workers. As in previous years, during Ramadan the HRC broadcast a public awareness program on television emphasizing the Islamic injunction to treat employees well.

The government did not always enforce the laws protecting migrant workers effectively. Many migrant workers were employed on terms to which they had not agreed and experienced problems, such as delays in the payment of wages, changes in employer, or changed working hours and conditions. Migrant workers, especially domestic workers, were vulnerable to abuse, exploitation, and conditions contravening labor laws, including nonpayment of wages, working for periods in excess of the 48-hour workweek, working for periods longer than the prescribed eight-hour workday, and restrictions on movement due to passport confiscation. There were also reports of physical and verbal abuse.

Many noncitizen workers, particularly domestic employees, were not able to exercise their right to remove themselves from dangerous situations. Some employers physically prevented workers from leaving or threatened them with nonpayment of wages if they left. Sponsoring employers, who controlled foreign workers' ability to remain employed and in the country, usually held foreign workers' passports, a practice prohibited by law. In some contract disputes, a sponsor held the employee in the country until resolution of the dispute to force the employee to accept a disadvantageous settlement or risk deportation without any settlement.

Foreign workers could contact the labor offices of their embassies for assistance. During the year hundreds of domestic workers, the majority of whom were female, sought shelter at their embassies, some fleeing sexual abuse or other violence by their employers. Some embassies maintained safe houses for citizens fleeing situations that amounted to bondage. The workers usually sought legal help from embassies and government agencies to obtain end-of-service benefits and exit visas.

In addition to their embassies, domestic servants could contact the NSHR, the HRC, the governmental Interministerial General Secretariat to Combat Human Trafficking, and the Migrant Workers' Welfare Department of the Ministry of Labor, which provided services to safeguard migrant workers' rights and protect them from abuse. Workers could also apply to the offices of regional governors and lodge an appeal with the Board of Grievances against decisions by those authorities.